VENETIAN REPUBLIC

Nino Zoccali

Nino Zoccali

VENETIAN REPUBLIC

Recipes from the Veneto,
Adriatic Croatia, and the Greek islands

Interlink Books

An imprint of Interlink Publishing Group, Inc.
Northampton, Massachusetts

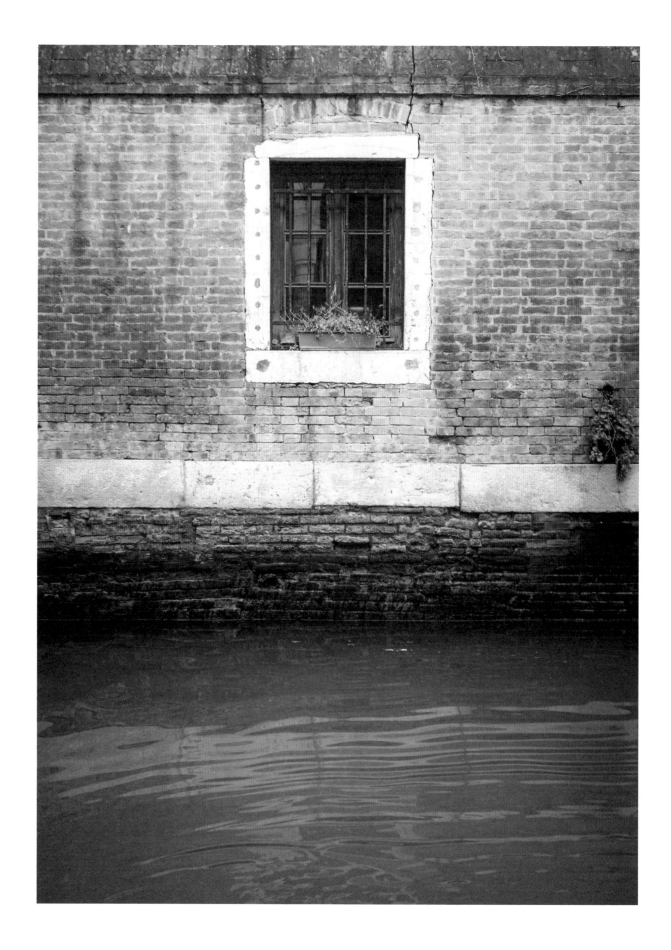

CONTENTS

ABOUT NINO

Nino Zoccali grew up in rural Western Australia surrounded by quality produce. His mother came from a family who have farmed in the region for almost 100 years. His father, a first-generation Italian immigrant, grew, harvested, reared, or bartered for just about everything that was ever placed on the dinner table—from artisanal homemade charcuterie and tomato *sugo*, to the highest quality home-grown meats and vegetables. It was at this table that Nino's love for Italian cuisine began.

After completing a double major degree in Economics and Italian, Nino went on to pursue a career in the culinary arts. At 25, he opened his first restaurant, Caffe Contadino, in Margaret River, Australia, to critical acclaim. In 1998, Nino moved to Sydney, and not long afterwards he headed the opening team at Otto Ristorante Italiano on Woolloomooloo wharf.

Today, Nino and his wife, Krissoula, own and operate two of Australia's most loved and highly awarded Italian restaurants: The Restaurant Pendolino and La Rosa The Strand. Both restaurants reside in the stunning, heritage-listed Strand Arcade in Sydney, and boast a loyal clientele of business, political, and fashion elite.

Nino is also a passionate olive oil and wine expert, and his first cookbook, *Pasta Artigiana*, was published in 2012.

LA SERENISSIMA

My fascination with Venice goes back a long way. Many years ago, when I was just 21 and had completed a 12-month sabbatical in Southern Italy, I found myself on my way to London. I had a little time on my hands, so I asked my learned older cousin, Liliana Di Certo, for advice on what I thought would be a difficult question—where should my next stop in Italy be? I'd been to Rome and Milan several times, but hadn't ventured far beyond those cities or the southern region of Calabria, the birthplace of my father. "Liliana, I only have a few days. Where do you think I should go: Florence or Venice?"

She didn't hesitate. "Venice. You are going to Venice and I am going to organize it. In Florence, you have to line up to see the art. Yes, it's amazing when you get in and see it, but in Venice, *everything* is art. There's art inside and outside, everywhere you look. It's one of the most unique places in the entire world and the barrier of water has preserved her history like nowhere else. You are going to Venice."

And so my obsession with the floating city was born. Little did I know that Venice would continue to lure and inspire me for decades to come. Since my first visit as a wide-eyed Italo–Australian boy from Bunbury, Western Australia, I've built a career as an Italian chef and restaurateur, and returned frequently. Along the way I've also fostered a keen interest in art, music, and history, and nowhere in the world are these more beautifully represented and nurtured than in Venice.

Made up of 118 islands, Venice is the jewel of the Mediterranean. "An archaeological site which still breathes life," according to UNESCO, which rightly added Venice and her lagoons to its World Heritage Sites list in 1987. "Venice is a unique artistic achievement ... In this unreal space, where there is no notion of the concept of 'terra ferma,' masterpieces of one of the most extraordinary architectural museums on Earth have been accumulated for over 1000 years."

Putting aside population growth and a booming tourism trade, the Venice of today isn't vastly different from the Venice of the Middle Ages and Renaissance. The water that surrounds her keeps Venice separate from her neighbors, something that Venetians—a fiercely independent people—aren't perturbed by in the slightest. This spiritual and geographical independence has kept the romance of the city alive and well for generations. Venice is a floating cultural incubator. A living fossil.

But my obsession with Venice is about more than just her artistic and architectural blessings. It's about how it all came to be. How did such a small place grow to not only enjoy such unrivaled opulence, but also play a defining role in shaping the culture and cuisine of her Mediterranean neighbors? Many are unaware that Venice had a completely transformative effect on regions along the Adriatic Sea—an effect that is still very much apparent today, some 13 centuries after Venice rose to prominence.

What makes Venice's revered status so remarkable is the fact that it was born from desperation. Venice was founded in AD 421, after refugees from Roman cities including Padua, Aquileia, Treviso, Altino, and Concordia fled Barbarian conquerors for her relative safety, where they used the marshy lagoon for protection. They joined the *incolae lacunae*, or "lagoon dwellers," fishermen who made a living from the fruits of the waters.

Venice's location at the head of the Adriatic Sea, with her countless canals and waterways, ensured she was well protected from attack or invasion. But the people's proficiency on water and their unrivaled artistry in shipbuilding put Venice in a unique position, where, despite her size and population, she became an incredible facilitator of trade.

And so the Venetian Republic was born. Existing for the millennia between the 8th and 18th centuries, the Venetian Republic refers to the thalassocracy—or empire at sea—that saw Venice dominate the trade routes on the Adriatic Sea, including commerce between Europe and North Africa. The wealth generated by this dominance created the Venice we know today.

Acclaimed food writer Waverley Root, whose 1971 book *The Food of Italy* is my bible on the history of Italian cooking, scribes:

The free state of Venice maintained its independence for a thousand years. Its power extended inland over all northeastern Italy, and along the valley of the Po into part of what is now Lombardy; and for some 200 years it was the world's greatest maritime power. From fishermen, the Venetians had become sailors. From coastal traders, they had become navigators, sailing especially toward the ports of the Levant. From dealers with the East by sea, they became importers from the East by land...

And so the great water-trading empire came to largely monopolize East–West trade for generations.

The importance of water in Venice's ascent cannot be underestimated. It was on water where the Venetians were most comfortable, and where their influence was most apparent. As such, the waterways throughout the Venetian Republic became the superhighways of the era, where culinary staples such as salt, pepper, spices, corn, and grain were traded, and via which cultural and intellectual ideas were exchanged. Water was Venice's competitive advantage, and the medium through which her artistic and fiscal wealth were born.

Venetians' lives are built around water, both literally and figuratively—from around AD 1000 the annual Marriage of the Sea ceremony saw the ruling leader, or Doge, throw a ring into the sea and vow, "We wed thee, sea, as a sign of true and everlasting domination." This tradition continues today.

The Venetian Republic is often romantically referred to as *La Serenissima*, or "the most serene Republic." This has nothing to do with Venice's picturesque landscape or the calming effect of the water, but rather typifies the Venetians' motivations during their reign. They didn't rape, pillage, and conquer (at least not as much as other empires); they didn't want to acquire land aggressively or show the world that they were crusaders. They just wanted to make a lot of money from high-margin trading, and reinvest it back home to create an artistic icon. And this was all done, rather uniquely for the time, under the regime of a Republic, led by the Doge—an elected leader chosen by the elite classes of society at the time.

Like water, salt was fundamental in Venice's rise to glory. Venetians produced it from their copious briny lagoons, then sold it at an inflated price around the world. This monopoly allowed the Republic to buy meat from her neighbors; corn, originally from the Americas; rice, which was harvested in the marshy wetlands near the Po River; and exotic spices from the Arab countries of the East.

As they traded and sailed down the Adriatic, Venetians learned about new foods, crops, and cooking techniques, and incorporated them into their own cuisine, while also sharing them with their neighbors. Saffron, for example, came to Venice from the East and was then diffused throughout the Veneto. Polenta—an inescapable element of Mediterranean cuisine today—also came from the East, primarily from Turkey (one name for corn in Italian is *granoturco*—Turkish grain), and was exported back down the coast all the way to the Greek islands. But the use of fish is probably the most glaring example of the Venetian Republic's influence. Take cod, for instance...

In 1431 a Venetian ship left Crete, headed for the North Sea and Flanders, and was hit by a storm that ultimately saw the captain, Pietro Querini, and 14 of his crew taking refuge on the uninhabited rock of Sandøy, in Norway's northern Lofoten islands. For four months, the Venetians lived with Norwegian fishermen, and learned the art of preserving cod. Querini returned to Venice with 60 dried stockfish and showed the Doges how the Norwegians dried the fish in the wind, then beat and spiced it, turning it into a soft and tasty paste. The recipe was known by the Spanish words *baccalà mantecato*, and Querini returned to Norway many times, becoming a major trader in dried and salted codfish. Today, *baccalà mantecato* is a quintessential Venetian dish. You'll see this iteration in the Veneto too, as well as *baccalà alla vicentina*, salted codfish braised with onions, anchovies, and milk. Along the Croatian coast, *bakalar* is a salted cod stew with potatoes, always cooked and eaten on Christmas Eve. Head to the Greek islands and you'll find *bakaliaros*—salted cod, fried in a beer batter and used in savory pies.

Another dish threaded throughout the territories of *La Serenissima* is *pastissada*. It's true that seafood dominated (and continues to dominate) the cuisines of Venice, the Veneto, the Croatian coast, and throughout the Greek islands, but this meat stew has a number of interpretations throughout these territories. Venice's version, believed to have originated in Verona, uses red meat and wine—traditionally horse meat and red wine of the Valpolicella—neither of which she could produce herself. Croatia (which claims *pašticada* as its national dish) and Greece incorporate spices such as cloves, pepper, cinnamon, paprika, and nutmeg—the fruits of the Republic's trade with the Ottoman Empire.

In this book I've decided to focus on the four key regions that geographically encapsulate the Venetian Republic, and which each have their own distinct cuisine, albeit with undeniable Venetian influences. These are Venice and her lagoon islands; the Veneto, of which Venice is the capital; the Croatian coast; and the Greek islands formerly under Venetian rule. I've selected dishes with strong Venetian roots or influence and have taken poetic license with some of the interpretations to give them a more modern treatment, celebrating ingredients and techniques that show how, to this day, the food in this magnificent region continues to be influenced by foreign forces.

Call it fate or serendipity, but these regions managed to weave their way into both my personal and professional life long before the concept for this book came to fruition. My business partner and wife of 18 years, Krissoula Syrmis, is from Ithaca, a Greek island that became part of the Republic in the 16th century. Cristian Casarin, our restaurant group sommelier, whose first desk was a milk crate and who's worked by my side since day one, grew up in the Veneto town of Noale. One of my dearest friends, Ino Kuvacic, an amazing Croatian chef, and his wonderful wife, Mariana, continue to espouse the essential culinary link between Venetian and Croatian coastal cooking. My love for Venice and the Venetian Republic has been fed by these wonderful relationships, and I am so grateful for the culinary and cultural insights shared with me over what already feels like a lifetime.

THE VENETIAN REPUBLIC

DURING THE FIFTEENTH CENTURY

Black Sea

OTTOMAN

CONSTANTINOPLE

EMPIRE

Aegean Sea

ATHENS

Greece

SANTORINI

CRETE

CYPRUS

VENICE

I

FROM REFUGE TO REPUBLIC

The story of Venice is an extraordinary one, and the people who have shaped the city are unique. Entrepreneurial, tenacious, strategic, and, possibly above all, proud. Throughout history they have been a people determined to see their home become unlike any other place in the world. As I mentioned in the introduction, the original Venetian "lagoon dwellers" were joined by others seeking refuge from Barbarian invaders, and together they set about converting this marshland into the epicenter of an empire—a cultural leader beyond comparison. The Venetians wanted Venice to be a global city, and they used the wealth generated from their high-margin trading to do this, cultivating a society brimming with artistic talent and delight as they went. To my favorite author on this—Waverley Root:

The Venetians created a brilliant society with the riches brought them by spices and commerce. Was it the effect of the exotic nature of their merchandise? "The intellectual faculties seem to have soared in an enduring exaltation under the influence of spices," Alexandre Dumas wrote in his Grand Dictionnaire de Cuisine. "Is it to spices that we owe [the great Venetian] Titian's masterpieces? I am tempted to believe it." Yet the Genoese dealt in spices too. They were rich too. Yet when they decided to spend their money on art, they had to seek painters elsewhere. The Venetians developed their own artists.

By the 12th century, the Venetians were proud to be building an empire that was rapidly becoming the envy of the world, and Venice was their showpiece—a celebration of the greatest things humanity could buy, sell, and, most importantly, create. Venice was becoming a center of investment in art and culture and a place of cultivation for the finest things imaginable.

As one of the first international trading giants and then one of the first major tourist destinations in the world, Venice has never hesitated to take the best of what she has access to and use it to create something unique. Of course, this is more than evident in her cooking. Key trading commodities from the Ottoman Empire, including pepper, cloves, cinnamon, ginger, and nutmeg, were embraced by Venice, then traded with the rest of Europe, but not before being used to help form new and exciting dishes that would go on to be considered classically Venetian.

Take *sarde in saor*, for example. While fish was historically seen as sustenance for the poor in Venice, these sweet-and-sour sardines, and similar dishes, are today a pillar of Venetian cooking. Key to the dish are pine nuts and raisins—imports from the East. *Pincia*, Venice's version of a bread pudding, is made from dried fruits, eggs, milk, and usually dried bread, as well as cinnamon and nutmeg, also courtesy of the East.

If fish was the food of the lower classes, then meat—particularly game birds— was exclusively for society's upper echelons. But where did it come from? Not the East, but the Veneto to the North, where the people were far more proficient in rearing land-based proteins than their Venetian rulers, for obvious reasons. Roast duck, veal liver with onions, and both beef and equine versions of slow-cooked *pastissada* are today considered as Venetian as any dish will ever be.

Venetians are proud, but this pride has always been balanced with a willingness to admit that Venice has taken many cultural cues from her neighbors. Despite being fiercely patriotic, most Venetians will still tell you that their home has always been an international city in some way. Indeed, Venice represents everything she has touched, while she has also uniquely touched the rest of the world. Where in the Western world (and probably most of the East as well) has one not heard of Venetian glass or Venetian blinds or Vivaldi's *Four Seasons* or of two of Shakespeare's most famous masterpieces: *Othello* and *The Merchant of Venice*? Carnevale and mask-making was, and is, Venice. Where did Hemingway, Casanova, and Marco Polo live? And who isn't aware of the Venice Film Festival and Biennale?

It's the same with food and wine. It's no coincidence that Venice lays claim to being the birthplace of the modern-day café—Florian—the first and oldest continually trading coffee house in the world (save for the interruption of a couple of world wars). She is also home to arguably the most famous restaurant on the planet over the past century—Harry's Bar—home of carpaccio and the bellini. And let's not forget prosecco, the Veneto's international juggernaut sparkling appellation wine, made famous in Venice, and now the best-selling sparkling wine in the world.

What about produce? While boutique in size, Venice's Rialto boasts one of the world's best retail food markets. Take a short boat trip to Chioggia, or "little Venice" as it is often referred, and you'll find Italy's largest wholesale and retail fish markets.

To the deep weight of trade-driven foreign ingredients, one really needs to add another interesting impact on the cooking of Venice—that of the centuries-old influence of elite international hotel cuisine, which has become part of the culinary fabric of Venice, at times feeling more classically French than traditionally Italian. The common use of ingredients such as curry powder, mayonnaise, and Cognac sets Venice apart from most places in Italy and is fortified by centuries of international hotel operations and tourism. Lobster thermidor, oysters Rockefeller, scampi americaine, and beef Wellington are not uncommon throughout modern history across the lagoon isles.

Venice is all of this.

Antipasti

FISH AND SHELLFISH CARPACCIO

Prep Time 25 minutes

2 tablespoons pistachios
3 oz (80 g) swordfish fillet
3 oz (80 g) tuna fillet
3 oz (80 g) scallops
4 large scampi/langoustines
  (or large shrimp)
½ pomegranate
2 tablespoons lemon juice
½ cup (120 ml) Agrumato lemon
  extra virgin olive oil
2 tablespoons salmon roe
Sea salt and freshly ground
  black pepper

Named after Vittore Carpaccio, the Renaissance painter famous for his use of vivid colors, the original carpaccio dish was first plated at the iconic Harry's Bar in Venice—one of the most famous restaurants in history. At Harry's, the carpaccio has always been a raw beef dish, deeply tied to Venice and her cultural history; however, carpaccio is an apt description for any raw dish *(crudo)*.

Preheat the oven to 325°F (170°C). Arrange the pistachios evenly on a baking sheet and roast for 6–8 minutes, or until lightly browned. Take out of the oven and remove the nuts from the sheet to prevent them over-coloring. Allow to cool completely before roughly chopping.

To prepare the fish and shellfish, remove any skin and blood lines. Peel the scampi, then cut in half and devein: do this by using a toothpick to pierce at the back of the head to a depth of a few millimeters, then lift up the end of the toothpick to scoop out the alimentary vein. Pull the vein gently to remove.

Finely slice the swordfish, tuna, and scallops and arrange on individual plates. Add two scampi halves to each plate.

Remove the seeds from the pomegranate by holding it over a bowl, seed-side down, and tapping on the skin side of the fruit with a wooden spoon. The seeds will fall out. Remove any white pith from the seeds and scatter them over the carpaccio.

Scatter the pistachios over the carpaccio. Combine the lemon juice and extra virgin olive oil in a small bowl, and dress the carpaccio.

Scatter the salmon roe over the top, and season with sea salt and pepper.

—Serves 4

MIXED VENETIAN CROSTINI

This is classic *bacari* (wine bar food), served in any one of the multitude of hole-in-the-wall wine bars in Venice. A very Venetian tradition is to enjoy these bite-sized crostini during the late-afternoon *aperitivo* hour, when couples, friends, and worn-out tourists round out the day with a selection of *cicchetti* (snacks) and *ombrette* (little glasses of regional wine). A tradition worth savoring, I say.

BACCALA MANTECATO

Prep Time 15 minutes, plus 48 hours for cod preparation
Cooking Time 35 minutes

13½ oz (380 g) salt cod (*baccala*)
1 garlic clove
1 bay leaf
Generous ¾ cup (200 ml) extra virgin olive oil,
    plus extra for brushing crostini
2 tablespoons lemon juice
1 thin Italian baguette
8 black olives, roughly chopped
1 tablespoon lemon zest
1 tablespoon finely chopped parsley
Freshly ground black pepper

—Serves 4

Wash the excess salt from the salt cod and then soak it in cold water in the fridge for 48 hours, changing the water twice each day. This process will remove most of the fish's saltiness. After 48 hours, remove the fish and pat it dry with paper towels.

Place the fish, garlic, and bay leaf in a large pot and cover with water. Cook over medium heat for 30 minutes. Drain and set aside, discarding the fish skin, bones, and bay leaf.

Using a food processor, blend the fish to a paste, slowly adding the extra virgin olive oil in a steady stream to emulsify. Add the lemon juice and season with pepper (no salt needed).

Slice the baguette into ½ inch (1 cm) slices on an angle, brush with olive oil, and toast until crisp under a broiler or in a cast-iron skillet on the stovetop.

Generously spread the *baccala* onto the crostini, then place the chopped olives on top and garnish with lemon zest and parsley.

TINY SHRIMP AND MAYONNAISE

Prep Time 15 minutes
Cooking Time 5 minutes

14 oz (400 g) small shrimp, cooked and peeled
Scant ½ cup (3½ oz/100 g) Mayonnaise (page 241)
1 teaspoon Worcestershire sauce
1 tablespoon lemon juice
½ teaspoon lemon zest
¼ cup (½ oz/15 g) chopped chives
1 thin Italian baguette
Extra virgin olive oil, for brushing crostini
Sea salt and freshly ground black pepper

—Serves 4

Combine the shrimp with the mayonnaise, Worcestershire sauce, lemon juice, zest, and chives and season with salt and pepper.

Slice the baguette into ½ inch (1 cm) slices on an angle, brush with the olive oil, and toast until crisp under a broiler or in a cast-iron skillet on the stovetop.

Place the shrimp mayonnaise mixture on top of the crostini and serve.

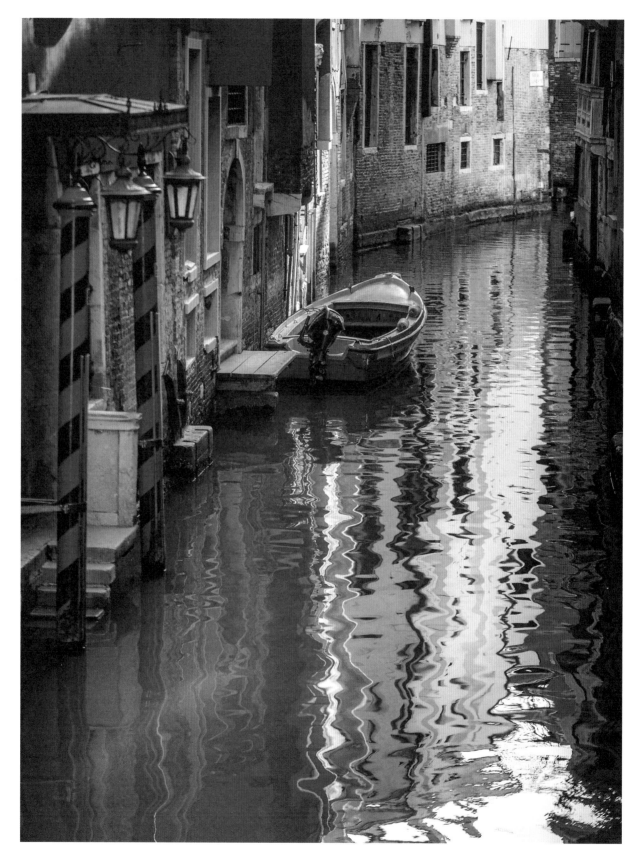

SARDINES "IN SAOR"

Prep Time 10 minutes
Cooking Time 20 minutes

Scant ½ cup (2 oz/60 g) pine nuts
½ cup (130 ml) extra virgin olive oil,
    plus extra for brushing crostini
8 sardine fillets
½ cup (3 oz/80 g) sliced onions
⅓ cup (70 ml) white wine
¼ cup (60 ml) white wine vinegar
1 pinch cinnamon
2 bay leaves
1 sprig thyme
⅓ cup (2 oz/60 g) raisins
1 thin Italian baguette

—Serves 4

Preheat the oven to 325°F (170°C). Arrange the pine nuts evenly on a baking sheet and roast for 6–8 minutes, or until lightly browned. Take out of the oven and remove the nuts from the sheet to prevent them over-coloring. Allow to cool completely before using.

Heat the olive oil in a large frying pan over medium heat for 1 minute, then add the sardines and cook for 1 minute on each side. Remove from the pan and place on a serving platter.

Add the onion to the frying pan and cook over low heat for 10 minutes to soften. Add the wine, vinegar, cinnamon, bay leaves, thyme, and raisins and cook for 4 minutes, then pour over the sardines and allow to completely cool.

Slice the baguette into ½ inch (1 cm) slices on an angle, brush with olive oil, and toast until crisp under a broiler or in a cast-iron skillet on the stovetop.

Top the crostini with the sardines *in saor* and garnish with pine nuts.

SCALLOP AND CASTELLUCCIO LENTILS

Prep Time 10 minutes
Cooking Time 30 minutes

1 garlic clove, minced
1 bay leaf
1 sprig rosemary
½ onion, diced
1⅓ cups (330 ml) extra virgin olive oil,
    plus extra for brushing crostini
¾ cup (5½ oz/150 g) Castelluccio (or French Puy) lentils
½ tomato, finely diced
3½ oz (100 g) celery, finely diced
14 oz (400 g) medium-sized scallops
¼ cup (½ oz/15 g) finely chopped parsley
Scant ½ cup (100 ml) lemon juice
1 thin Italian baguette
Sea salt and freshly ground black pepper

—Serves 4

In a saucepan, sauté the garlic, bay leaf, rosemary, and onion in generous ¾ cup (200 ml) of the olive oil for 5 minutes or until the onion is translucent. Add the lentils and tomato and cover with water.

Cook the lentils over medium heat for 20–25 minutes, until tender but not mushy, topping up with water if needed. Drain the lentils, remove the tomato skins, bay leaf and rosemary, and chill in the fridge.

Blanch the celery in boiling water for 10 seconds, then refresh in ice water. Drain and mix with the lentils.

Heat a sauté pan with 1½ tablespoons of the olive oil over high heat for 1 minute, then add the scallops and sear quickly for 1 minute, caramelizing both sides. Add the scallops to the lentil mix, then add the parsley, lemon juice, and remaining olive oil and season.

Slice the baguette into ½ inch (1 cm) slices on an angle, brush with olive oil, and toast until crisp under a broiler or in a cast-iron skillet on the stovetop.

Top the crostini with the lentils and scallops and serve.

MIXED VENETIAN SANDWICHES

Like the Venetian crostini, this is another classic *bacari* dish. However, in true Venetian style, these are not humble sandwiches. Bulging with a double filling in the middle and often including some of Venice's most prized ingredients, these *cicchetti* are simple but indulgent, and are best enjoyed as the sun goes down with a little glass of Garganaga or Valpolicella. Life doesn't get much better.

SHRIMP, RICOTTA, AND PARSLEY TRAMEZZINI

Prep Time 5 minutes

7 oz (200 g) shrimp meat, cooked and cut
   into ½ inch (1 cm) cubes
Scant 1 cup (7 oz/200 g) ricotta cheese
2 tablespoons chopped parsley
½ tablespoon lemon zest
3 tablespoons Mayonnaise (page 241)
8 slices white bread
Sea salt and freshly ground black pepper

—Serves 4

Combine the cubed shrimp, ricotta, parsley, lemon zest, mayonnaise, and salt and pepper in a mixing bowl.

Cut the crusts off the bread. Lay four slices of bread on your work surface and place a quarter of the filling in the middle of each.

Place another slice of bread on top of each and, using both hands, press down on all sides to seal and form a bulging center. Cut the sandwiches in half crosswise.

TUNA, CAPER, AND CASTELFRANCO RADICCHIO TRAMEZZINI

Prep Time 10 minutes
Cooking Time 15 minutes

14 oz (400 g) tuna belly
Extra virgin olive oil, to coat the fish
1 oz (30 g) anchovies, finely chopped
¼ cup (1½ oz/40 g) capers
½ cup (3 oz/80 g) finely diced red onion
⅓ cup (¾ oz/20 g) finely chopped parsley
2 cups (4 oz/120 g) finely shredded Castelfranco radicchio
   (or Belgian endive)
5 tablespoons Mayonnaise (page 241)
8 slices white bread
Sea salt and freshly ground black pepper

—Serves 4

Preheat the oven to 315°F (160°C).

Rub the whole piece of tuna well with olive oil, place on a baking sheet, and bake for 15 minutes. Allow to cool.

Break the tuna apart into small pieces with your hands and combine with the anchovies, capers, onion, parsley, radicchio, and mayonnaise. Season with salt and pepper.

Cut the crusts off the bread. Lay four slices of bread on your work surface and place a quarter of the filling in the middle of each.

Place another slice of bread on top of each and, using both hands, press down on all sides to seal and form a bulging center. Cut the sandwiches in half crosswise.

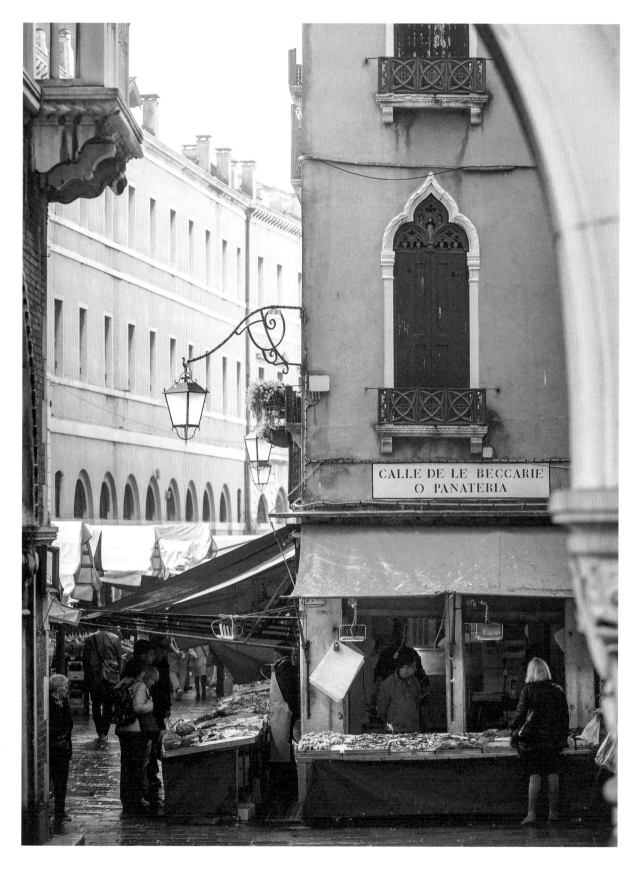

MORTADELLA, QUAIL EGG, AND WILD ARUGULA TRAMEZZINI

Prep Time 10 minutes
Cooking Time 4 minutes

12 quail eggs
8 slices white bread
3 tablespoons Mayonnaise (page 241)
7 oz (200 g) sliced mortadella
3 oz (80 g) wild arugula
Sea salt and freshly ground black pepper

—Serves 4

Bring a small pot of water to a boil. Gently place the quail eggs in the water and cook for 4 minutes. Drain, then chill in ice water. Peel and slice the eggs.

Cut the crusts off the bread. Lay four slices of bread on your work surface and spread thinly with mayonnaise. Divide the mortadella among the sandwiches, then add the arugula and eggs. Season with salt and pepper.

Spread the other four slices of bread thinly with mayonnaise. Place these slices on top of the others to make sandwiches. Using both hands, press down on all sides to seal and form a bulging center. Cut the sandwiches in half crosswise.

SPIDER CRAB AND MAYONNAISE TRAMEZZINI

Prep Time 4 minutes
Cooking Time 5 minutes

10½ oz (300 g) cooked spider crab meat (or any quality freshly cooked crab meat)
5 tablespoons Mayonnaise (page 241)
1 bunch chives, half left whole, half finely chopped
8 slices white bread
Sea salt and freshly ground black pepper

—Serves 4

Mix together the crab, mayonnaise, chopped chives, and salt and pepper.

Cut the crusts off the bread. Lay four slices of bread on your work surface and use an eighth of the filling on each slice of bread. Place the whole chives on top of the filling, then place the remaining filling on top of the chives, making a mound in the middle of each slice of bread.

Place another piece of bread on top of each and, using both hands, press down on all sides to seal and form a bulging center. Cut the sandwiches in half crosswise.

Notes
Fresh cooked crab meat can be bought or ordered from quality fishmongers.

The bread crusts can be processed into breadcrumbs and used to make meatballs, coat schnitzel or fish, or sprinkled over roasted vegetables.

VENETIAN-STYLE RENAISSANCE OYSTERS
with MIXED CAVIARS, LEMON JUICE, AND OLIVE OIL

Prep Time 5 minutes

Juice of ½ lemon, seeds removed
Generous ½ cup (150 ml)
    extra virgin olive oil
16 oysters
1 tablespoon salmon caviar
1 tablespoon trout caviar
1 tablespoon scampi caviar
    (or any caviar)
1 tablespoon sturgeon
    black caviar

This is not a dish that you'll find in Venice today, but it was prevalent in the Renaissance period, when caviar was sourced from sturgeon in the Po River and served as a luxurious garnish on oysters. At the time, Po River caviar was processed differently to how it is done nowadays, being gently cooked and then stored under oil. Lemon juice was also incorporated with the caviar in this dish, and left for a few hours before serving. Today this would be considered blasphemous as the acidity breaks down caviar—such a luxurious and expensive ingredient—which is why we suggest adding lemon juice immediately before serving. You're welcome to use as many or as few different caviars as you can source, but the colorful palette of this recipe makes it the perfect visual representation of the floating city's opulence and excess.

Mix together the lemon juice and extra virgin olive oil to make a dressing.

Top each oyster with ½ teaspoon of caviar, using different types on different oysters. Dress with a drizzle of lemon dressing just before serving.

Arrange the oysters on a large serving platter, alternating the caviars for an impressive presentation.

—Serves 4

Pasta, rice, and pies

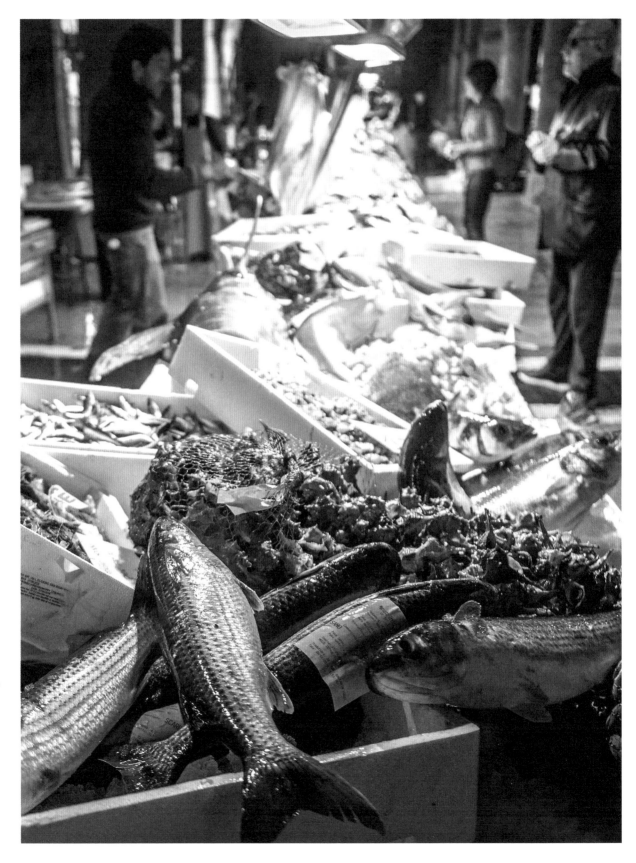

HEMINGWAY'S SCAMPI REMEDY RISOTTO

Prep Time 25 minutes
Cooking Time 2 hours

1 lb 5 oz (600 g) scampi/
langoustines (or large shrimp),
plus 2 whole scampi to serve as
a garnish (optional)
½ cup (120 ml) extra virgin
olive oil, plus extra for
the grilled scampi
1 tablespoon chopped parsley
½ teaspoon thyme leaves
4 cups (1 liter) Fish Stock
(page 236)
3½ oz (100 g) French shallots,
finely diced
1½ cups (11 oz/320 g) Vialone
Nano rice (or any risotto rice)
1 tablespoon Cognac or quality
brandy
1 cup (250 ml) white wine
6 tablespoons (3 oz/80 g) butter
Sea salt and freshly ground
black pepper

Bisque
4 tablespoons (2 oz/60 g)
butter
Scant ¼ cup (50 ml) olive oil
1 carrot, roughly chopped
1¼ cups (7 oz/200 g) roughly
chopped onion
1 celery stalk, roughly chopped
2½ oz (75 g) fennel bulb, chopped
8 garlic cloves, roughly chopped
6 parsley stems
6 thyme sprigs
1 fresh bay leaf
8 white peppercorns
6 tablespoons (3 oz/80 g) tomato
paste
Scant ¼ cup (50 ml) Cognac
or quality brandy
Generous ½ cup (150 ml)
dry white wine
1¼ cups (300 ml) light cream
4 cups (1 liter) Fish Stock
(page 236)
1 pinch cayenne pepper
Sea salt and freshly ground white
pepper

Ernest Hemingway, like so many other cultural icons, was deeply enamored with Venice. He was a regular at the city's famous institutions such as Harry's Bar—which actually featured in a couple of his works—and the luxurious Gritti Palace, where he always occupied the same seat. This recipe hung above that seat for many years. It's said that Hemingway self-prescribed this risotto to help alleviate pain from the injuries he sustained in two air crashes in Africa in the early 1950s.

Remove the heads and shells from the scampi and reserve to make the bisque. This will yield approximately 14 oz (400 g) of shells and 7 oz (200 g) of flesh.

To make the bisque, preheat the oven to 400°F (200°C). Mix together the butter and oil in a large mixing bowl. Crush the scampi shells and combine with the vegetables, garlic, herbs, bay leaf, peppercorns, and the butter and oil mixture. Season and mix well, then place in a roasting pan and roast in the oven, stirring frequently, until the vegetables are tender and the shells are golden brown. The aroma of the scampi shells should be prominent.

Transfer to a large pot and add all the remaining ingredients except the cayenne pepper. Bring to a boil over medium heat, reduce the heat to low, and simmer for between 60 and 90 minutes until the liquid is reduced by about half. Cool, then blend the ingredients in batches in a blender until smooth, and pass through a fine sieve. Season to taste with salt, white pepper, and cayenne pepper.

Devein the scampi by using a toothpick to pierce the back of the head to a depth of a few millimeters, then lift up the end of the toothpick to scoop out the alimentary vein. Pull the vein gently to remove. Cut the flesh into ½ inch (1 cm) pieces and mix with 1 tablespoon of the olive oil, parsley, and thyme.

Mix the fish stock and generous ¾ cup (200 ml) of the bisque together and bring to a boil, then simmer to maintain the heat as you will be adding this to the rice.

In a medium-sized saucepan over medium heat, heat the remaining olive oil with the shallots and cook for 3–4 minutes until translucent. Add the rice and cook for 2 minutes to toast the rice. Increase the heat, add the Cognac, and cook for 2 minutes. Add the wine and stir for 2 minutes or until it has evaporated.

Slowly start to add the hot fish stock and bisque one ladle at a time until the rice is al dente, stirring continually to create a creamy texture; this should take 15–20 minutes. When the rice is just cooked, add the scampi meat and stir through, then season with salt and pepper. Add the butter and stir through.

If serving with the additional grilled scampi, simply cut the scampi in half and remove the alimentary vein. Season with salt and pepper and drizzle with extra virgin olive oil. Broil or cook in a grill pan for 3–4 minutes or until just cooked, then arrange on top of the risotto on a serving platter.

—Serves 4

VENICE ✳ *Pasta, rice, and pies*

SPAGHETTI NERI *with* CASTRAURE ARTICHOKES AND CLAMS

Prep Time 10 minutes, plus overnight soaking
Cooking Time 35 minutes

1 lb 2 oz (500 g) clams
7 oz (200 g) castraure baby artichokes (or any baby artichokes)
14 oz (400 g) Squid (or Cuttlefish) Ink Fresh Egg Pasta Dough, cut into spaghetti (page 241)
6 tablespoons extra virgin olive oil
2 garlic cloves, minced
Scant ½ cup (100 ml) Sant'Erasmo Orto Istrian Malvasia (or any quality dry white wine)
¼ cup (½ oz/15 g) chopped Italian parsley
1 tablespoon (½ oz/15 g) butter, softened
Sea salt and freshly ground black pepper

Squid (and often cuttlefish) ink is a classic ingredient in Venetian cooking, as well as in the Veneto and throughout the Dalmatian coast. It's most commonly used to braise cuttlefish or calamari, mixed into pasta doughs, and stirred through risotto. In this recipe, we're partnering homemade squid ink spaghetti with two prized possessions from the Venetian island of Sant'Erasmo: baby purple artichokes and Istrian Malvasia wine, specifically Orto di Venezia, made by a revered winemaker from France, Thoulouze Michel, whose "natural" white wine is developing quite the cult following. Of course, any aromatic white can be used instead.

Place the clams in a container and cover with cold salted water. Refrigerate overnight to remove any sand and grit.

To cook the artichokes, simply put them whole in a pan of cold salted water and bring to a boil. Simmer for 10–20 minutes or until just cooked through to the center (you can check this with a skewer).

Once the artichokes are cooked, remove from the water and leave to cool; after that, they are very simply prepared by gently removing the outer leaves until you reach leaves that are tender enough to eat. Trim the base of each artichoke, removing the fibrous exterior. Set aside until ready to use (they are served whole).

Meanwhile, bring a large deep pot of salted water to a boil and cook the pasta until al dente.

Drain and rinse the clams well. In a medium-sized deep saucepan, heat the olive oil for 2 minutes, then add the garlic and cook for 1 minute. Turn up the heat to high and add the clams and wine and cook for 1 minute to release the alcohol from the wine. Next, place a lid on the pan and cook for a further 2 minutes, shaking the pan halfway through, until the clams open.

Add the artichokes and parsley to the pan and cook for another 2 minutes. Add the cooked pasta to the pan and season with salt and pepper, then stir in the softened butter. Serve on a large dish to share.

—Serves 4

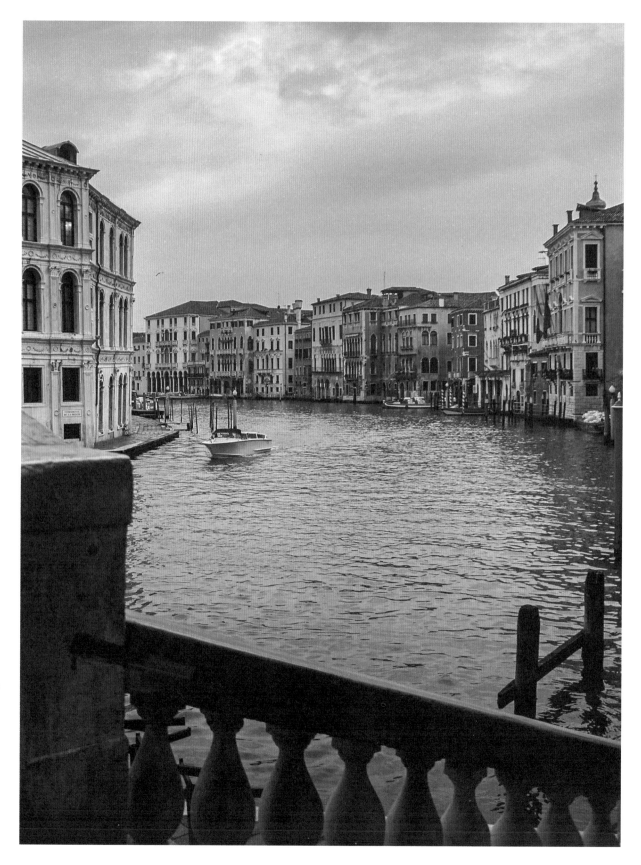

VENETIAN SPIDER CRAB PIE

Prep Time 45 minutes
Cooking Time 1 hour 20 minutes

14 oz (400 g) Fresh Egg Pasta
 Dough, rolled into sheets no
 thicker than ⅟₁₆ inch (1 mm)
 (page 240)
Generous ½ cup (150 ml)
 extra virgin olive oil
7 tablespoons (3½ oz/100 g)
 butter
1 cup (5½ oz/160 g) finely
 chopped onion
½ cup (2½ oz/70 g) finely diced
 fennel
2 garlic cloves, finely chopped
Generous ¾ cup (200 ml)
 white wine
4 cups (1 liter) tomato passata
 (puréed tomatoes)
½ bunch basil leaves
2 lb 4 oz (1 kg) cooked spider crab
 meat (or any quality fresh
 cooked crab meat)
7 oz (200 g) Parmigiano Reggiano
Sea salt and freshly ground
 black pepper

Béchamel sauce
4 cups (1 liter) milk
1 bay leaf
½ onion, diced
3 tablespoons (1½ oz/40 g) butter
⅓ cup (1½ oz/40 g) all-purpose
 flour
1 pinch nutmeg
Sea salt and freshly ground
 black pepper

Spider crab is one of Venice's most famous and abundant products. The crab flesh is absolutely stunning on its own—and Venetians enjoy it this way, usually as a main course. It's also really beautiful in this pie, which is commonly made—and also delicious—with a variety of different fish and crustaceans, not only spider crab.

Bring a pot of salted water to a boil and cook the pasta sheets until al dente, then drain. Pat dry with dish towels and set aside.

Place the extra virgin olive oil and butter in a medium-sized saucepan with the onion, fennel, and garlic and cook over low heat for 5 minutes, stirring regularly to make sure the vegetables do not take on any color. Add the white wine and cook again for 2 minutes, then add the tomato passata and basil leaves and season with salt and pepper. Cook for 25 minutes. When cool, fold the cooked crab meat into the sauce.

Preheat the oven to 350°F (180°C).

To make the béchamel sauce, bring the milk, bay leaf, and onion to a gentle simmer in a saucepan over medium heat. Strain, return the milk to the saucepan, and keep warm.

In another medium saucepan, melt the butter over low heat, then add the flour and mix to form a thick paste (roux). Cook for a further 3 minutes, stirring continuously. Slowly add the hot milk to the roux, stirring to create a smooth consistency, then season with salt, pepper, and nutmeg.

To build the pie, take a 12 × 6 inch (30 × 15 cm) baking dish and spread one ladle of béchamel sauce on the base, then add a layer of pasta sheets, then a layer of the crab mix. Continue layering in this sequence, finishing with a layer of béchamel sauce. Finely grate the Parmigiano over the top and bake for 45 minutes.

Note
Fresh cooked crab meat can be bought or ordered from quality fishmongers.

—Serves 6

SALT FISH AND SHRIMP RAVIOLI
with SAGE BROWN BUTTER AND SHRIMP REDUCTION

Prep Time 30 minutes, plus cod preparation and chilling
Cooking Time 1 hour 30 minutes

Salt cod
1 lb 2 oz (500 g) salt cod
(*baccala)* fillets
1 garlic clove
1 bay leaf

Ravioli filling
2 lb 4 oz (1 kg) shrimp, shells on
1¼ cups (10½ oz/300 g) ricotta
cheese
2 tablespoons chopped garlic
2¼ cups (3½ oz/100 g) baby
spinach
Scant ½ cup (100 ml) extra virgin
olive oil
Generous ½ cup (150 ml)
white wine
Sea salt and freshly ground
black pepper

Shrimp reduction
4 tablespoons extra virgin olive oil
1 onion, chopped
1 cup (5 oz/140 g) chopped celery
1 cup (5½ oz/160 g) chopped
carrot
2 garlic cloves, crushed
1 teaspoon chopped thyme
1 tablespoon tomato paste
1 cup (250 ml) white wine
1 bay leaf
3 black peppercorns
1 cup (250 ml) Fish Stock
(page 236)

Pasta
14 oz (400 g) Fresh Egg Pasta
Dough, rolled into sheets no
thicker than ⅟₁₆ inch (1 mm)
(page 240)
Semolina, for dusting
11 tablespoons (5½ oz/160 g)
butter
½ cup (⅓ oz/10 g) sage leaves

You may or may not find this dish in Venice, but what you won't struggle to find is salt cod, or *baccala*, most traditionally in the *mantecato* (whipped) form, but also in an array of other beautiful applications, like this one, where it's paired with the delicate taste and texture of shrimp. Making your own salt cod is relatively easy, and a great thing to do if you have an abundance of fish that you'd like to preserve. Store-bought salt cod can be lovely too—you just have to soak it in water in the fridge for a couple of days to alleviate the saltiness.

Wash the excess salt from the salt cod and then soak it in cold water in the fridge for 48 hours, changing the water twice each day. This process will remove most of the fish's saltiness. After 48 hours, remove and pat dry with paper towels. Finely chop the salt cod.

Place the salt cod, garlic, and bay leaf in a large saucepan, cover with water and cook over medium heat for 30 minutes. Drain, discarding the fish skin, bones, bay leaf, and garlic clove.

To make the ravioli filling, peel and devein the shrimp, keeping the shells and heads for the shrimp reduction.

Strain the ricotta in dish towels to remove all the liquid. Set aside.

Split the peeled shrimp, garlic, spinach, olive oil, and wine into three equal parts, keeping them separate. Place a third of the olive oil in a medium pan and bring to medium–high heat. Place one part of the garlic into the pan, then add one part of the shrimp and sauté until the garlic and shrimp are golden brown. Be careful not to burn the garlic. Place one part of the baby spinach into the pan and cook until the spinach has wilted. Deglaze the pan with one part of the white wine and place the mixture on a flat dish. Repeat this process until all the shrimp are cooked, then place the dish in the fridge until chilled.

Once cool, roughly process the shrimp and spinach in a food processor, then add the salt cod and process until thoroughly mixed. Place in a bowl, add the ricotta, and mix with a wooden spoon until fully incorporated. Season with salt and pepper.

To make the shrimp reduction, heat the olive oil in a medium-sized saucepan for 2 minutes, then add the reserved shrimp heads and shells, and cook over medium heat for 5 minutes. Add the onion, celery, carrot, garlic, and thyme and cook for a further 3 minutes.

continued...

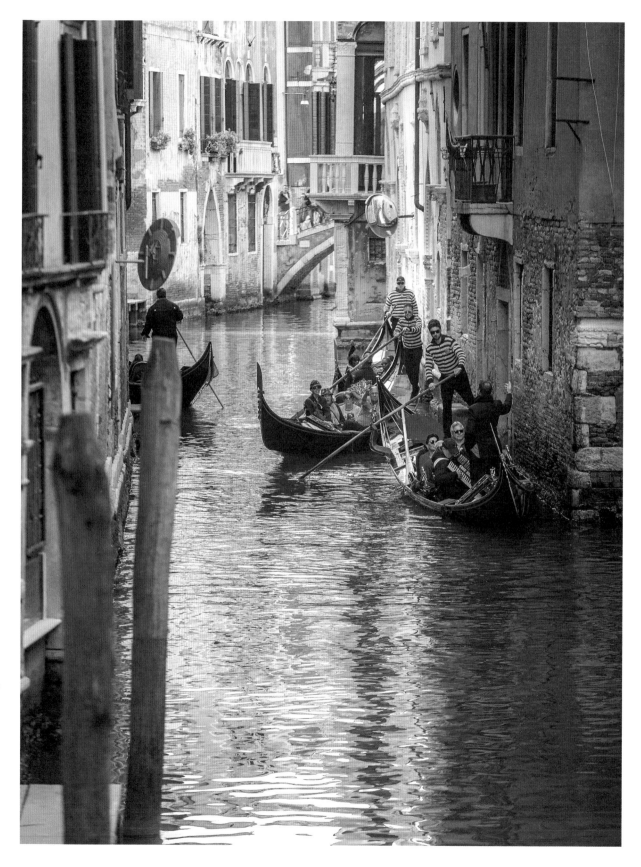

Add the tomato paste to the pan and stir through, then add the white wine, bay leaf, and peppercorns and cover with 1 cup (250 ml) water and the fish stock. Bring to a simmer and cook for 30 minutes.

Strain this shrimp broth through a fine strainer into a saucepan on the stovetop and simmer to reduce the liquid to a third of its original volume. Season with salt and pepper. Set aside.

Dust a piece of parchment paper with semolina. To make the ravioli, brush one sheet of the pasta dough lightly with water and place ½ tablespoon portions of the ravioli filling at 2 inch (5 cm) intervals. Place another sheet of pasta on top and press around the mixture to remove any air. Using a 2 inch (5 cm) cutter, cut round ravioli shapes around the filling and place them on the parchment paper.

Bring a large pot of salted water to a boil and gently place the ravioli in the boiling water. Cook for 2 minutes.

Add the butter and sage to a sauté pan and cook over low heat until the butter turns a nut brown color.

Toss the ravioli in the brown butter and then divide them among the serving dishes. Drizzle the shrimp reduction over the pasta.

—Serves 4

VENETIAN PROSECCO AND SNAPPER RISOTTO

Prep Time 30 minutes
Cooking Time 1 hour 30 minutes

1 × 3 lb 5 oz (1.5 kg) red snapper, filleted, bones chopped and washed and reserved for stock
3 garlic cloves, roughly chopped
6 tablespoons extra virgin olive oil, plus extra for frying the fish
3 tablespoons lemon juice
4½ cups (1.1 liters) Fish Stock (page 236)
½ cup (3 oz/80 g) finely diced French shallots
1¾ cups (12½ oz/350 g) Vialone Nano rice (or any risotto rice)
2 cups (500 ml) La Farra Prosecco DOCG (or any good prosecco)
6 tablespoons (3 oz/80 g) butter
Sea salt and freshly ground black pepper

Risotto can be made with any number of white-fleshed fish, but in Venice it's commonly made with red snapper. As with all risotto, the key is the quality of the stock, which is enriched here with the snapper bones. Another classic fish risotto, *risotto di gò*, utilizes whole small lagoon fish and cooks them until they almost completely dissolve. However, most foreigners, while appreciating the intense flavors of classic dishes like *risotto di gò*, don't understand how it can be a fish risotto without any visible fish in it. As such, I've done my best to please both the traditionalists and those who eat with their eyes, including seared snapper fillets so it not only looks more satisfying, but can also be served as a substantial main course.

In a deep pot, sauté the red snapper bones and half the garlic in half the olive oil. Add the lemon juice and stock and bring to a boil. Lower the heat and gently simmer for 45 minutes, skimming regularly. Strain, return to a clean pot, and keep at a simmer on the stovetop.

Cut the snapper fillets into four 5½ oz (150 g) pieces and, using a sharp knife, score the skin of the fish across the fillet in ½ inch (1 cm) intervals.

Heat the remaining olive oil in another saucepan over low heat for 1 minute. Add the shallots and remaining garlic and cook gently for 4 minutes until they are translucent. Add the rice and stir through, coating the rice with oil, then cook over high heat for a further 2 minutes. Add the prosecco to the rice and cook until the wine has evaporated.

Slowly add the hot stock to the rice, one ladle at a time, stirring continuously until it has been absorbed before adding the next ladle, until you have a creamy texture. This will take 15–20 minutes.

You will need to cook the snapper before the risotto is ready. Heat a little extra virgin olive oil in a non-stick frying pan over medium heat for 2 minutes. Season the snapper with salt and pepper on both sides and add to the pan, skin-side down. Gently press the top of each piece of fish with a spatula for 10 seconds so the skin of the fish is flat against the base of pan—this will make the skin crisp.

Cook the fish for approximately 7 minutes on the skin side, then turn over and cook again for a further 2 minutes (depending on its thickness). Set aside to rest for 1–2 minutes.

When the risotto is ready, season with salt and pepper. Add the butter on top without stirring, then cover and let the risotto rest for 2 minutes before stirring in the butter.

Divide the risotto among the serving plates and top with a snapper fillet.

—*Serves 4*

TAGLIOLINI PASTA *with* HOMEMADE BUTTER, WHITE ALBA TRUFFLE, AND PARMIGIANO REGGIANO

Prep Time 10 minutes
Cooking Time 10 minutes

14 oz (400 g) Fresh Egg Pasta Dough, cut into tagliolini (page 240)
scant 1 cup (7 oz/200 g) Homemade Butter (page 243)
4 tablespoons finely grated Parmigiano Reggiano, plus extra to serve
1½ oz (40 g) white Alba truffle, for slicing
Sea salt and freshly ground white pepper

A classic Northern Italian dish, this is also very much a staple of high-end Venetian dining. At the right times of year you'd be hard pressed to find a quality restaurant in Venice that isn't serving one version or another of this recipe. The white truffles are from Alba in Piedmont and, while not a Veneto product, they're regularly eaten across the whole of Northern Italy and are an absolute favorite in Venice and the Veneto, sitting alongside less-prized black truffles from other regions. This is a dish to savor.

Fill a large deep pot with water and bring to a boil. Season with 2 tablespoons salt, add the pasta, and bring back to a boil, then cook for 1–2 minutes. Drain the pasta, reserving a spoonful of the pasta water.

In a large sauté pan, gently melt the butter with the reserved pasta water over medium heat. Add the grated Parmigiano Reggiano, then add the cooked pasta and stir everything together. Season with salt and pepper to taste and stir again.

Serve on a large platter. Finely slice the truffle over the pasta and finish with a final grating of cheese.

—Serves 4

Mains

SEA PERCH "ACQUA PAZZA" BURANO STYLE
with SANT'ERASMO PROSECCO AND CHERRY TOMATOES

Prep Time 15 minutes
Cooking Time 20 minutes

Generous ¾ cup (200 ml) Lake Garda extra virgin olive oil (or any quality early-harvest extra virgin olive oil)
4 garlic cloves, thinly sliced
2 anchovies
1 × 1 lb 12 oz (800 g) sea perch (or ocean perch), cleaned, scaled, and gutted
9 oz (250 g) cherry tomatoes
1 tablespoon baby capers
½ cup (¾ oz/20 g) basil leaves
1 bay leaf
1⅔ cups (400 ml) Sant'Erasmo Prosecco (or any quality prosecco)
Freshly ground black pepper

Burano is a very famous Venetian fishing island that is a must-visit for any food-loving traveler. Fish served on the islands is the freshest of the fresh, coming in at all hours of the day. It doesn't get any better than at my favorite place to eat, a trattoria called Gatto Nero. Beautiful in its simplicity, this recipe hinges on the cooking of the fish, on the bone. If you get it right, the result will be beautiful and moist.

Preheat the oven to 400°F (200°C).

Place the olive oil, garlic, and anchovies in a large baking dish (or flame-safe baking sheet) on the stovetop over low heat and cook for 2 minutes, stirring occasionally.

Place the whole fish in the dish. Add the cherry tomatoes, capers, basil leaves, and bay leaf.

Pour the prosecco over the fish, cover with a lid or foil, and place in the oven for 10 minutes, then remove the lid or foil and cook for a further 5 minutes or until just cooked. Check the backbone at the head of the fish to see if it is cooked: the flesh should just be coming off the bone.

Season with black pepper and serve.

—Serves 2

LAGOON FISH AND SOFT SHELL CRAB FRITTO MISTO
with WHITE ASPARAGUS

Prep Time 40 minutes
Cooking Time 10 minutes

7 oz (200 g) calamari
8 white asparagus spears
8½ cups (2 liters) olive oil
1 egg, plus extra for egg wash
1 cup (250 ml) milk
5 cups (10½ oz/300 g) fresh
   breadcrumbs
½ cup (1 oz/30 g) chopped parsley
2 cups (10½ oz/300 g) all-purpose
   flour
7 oz (200 g) *moeche* (small
   soft shell crabs)
1 lb 5 oz (600 g) slip sole
   or flounder, cleaned,
   scaled, and deboned
7 oz (200 g) *schie* (school shrimp
   or bay shrimp), cooked, left
   whole and unpeeled
2 lemons, cut into wedges
Sea salt and freshly ground
   black pepper

Creamy horseradish sauce
1 cup (8½ oz/245 g) sour cream
¼ cup (¾ oz/20 g) grated fresh
   horseradish
1 tablespoon Dijon mustard
1 tablespoon white wine vinegar

Tartar sauce
1 egg yolk
1 tablespoon white wine vinegar
1 teaspoon Dijon mustard
Generous ¾ cup (200 ml)
   vegetable oil
2 tablespoons finely chopped
   French shallots
1 tablespoon chopped
   pickled cucumbers
2 tablespoons chopped capers
2 tablespoons chopped parsley
½ tablespoon lemon juice

One of the stars of this recipe is the *moeche*, or soft shell crab. An absolute delicacy in Venice—and boasting a suitable price tag—the little crustaceans are only available live for very short periods in autumn and spring. Despite occupying the Venetian lagoon all year round, they're only "*moeca*" for literally a matter of hours. During this time, the crabs molt, leaving their old shells behind in order to begin developing new and bigger ones. With very diligent fishermen watching on, the crabs are harvested at this critical time, without their shells, and rushed off to the local restaurants and produce markets— the ultimate, of course, being The Rialto Market. While *moeche* can be found snap-frozen (often the most accessible option outside Venice and the season), the classic preparation in Venice is not for the squeamish: live *moeche* are thrown into flour and fried until crispy and golden.

To make the horseradish sauce, whisk together all the ingredients.

To make the tartar sauce, whisk together the egg yolk, vinegar, and mustard. Slowly drizzle in the oil, whisking continuously to form a thick emulsion. Mix in the rest of the ingredients. Store in the fridge until needed.

To prepare the calamari, clean by removing the tentacles from the body and, using a knife, remove the hard beak from the center of the head. Reserve the head. With your fingers, pull the back bone, ink sac, and intestines out of the body, then peel the outer membrane/skin from the calamari and wash under cold running water. Leave whole or slice into ½ inch (1 cm) rings if the calamari is large.

Trim the asparagus, removing the woody base. You can test how far the woody section goes by bending the end of one spear and seeing where it breaks.

In a large deep pot or deep fryer, heat the olive oil to 350°F (180°C).

Beat the egg and milk in a mixing bowl to make an egg wash. In another bowl, mix the breadcrumbs and parsley and season with salt and pepper.

Crumb the asparagus by tossing it in flour, then in the egg wash, and finally in the breadcrumb mixture.

Cut the soft shell crabs in half, then pat dry with paper towels. Toss all the seafood separately in flour.

Starting with the larger fish (sole), place into the hot olive oil. The sole should take approximately 5 minutes to cook. After 3 minutes you can add the smaller fish, crab, school shrimp, and calamari. After about 2 minutes, remove the seafood from the oil and drain on paper towels. Season with salt and pepper.

Fry the asparagus in the hot oil until golden brown. Season with salt.

Serve the *fritto misto* on a platter with lemon wedges, the creamy horseradish sauce, and tartar sauce.

Notes
Soft shell crabs range in size from about 1½ inches (4 cm) to 4½ inches (12 cm). If the soft shell crabs are wider than 2½ inches (6 cm), they need to be cut in half. If not, leave them whole. In either case, the crabs need to be patted dry with a paper towel to remove as much water as possible before being tossed through flour, prior to frying. This is really important to ensure a crispy result.

This recipe makes more horseradish sauce and tartar sauce than is needed here. Store the remainder in airtight containers in the fridge for up to 2 weeks.

—Serves 4

STEAMED SHELLFISH *with* SANT'ERASMO CASTRAURE BABY ARTICHOKES AND ISOLA DELLE ROSE EXTRA VIRGIN OLIVE OIL

Prep Time 30 minutes, plus overnight soaking of clams, if using
Cooking Time 30 minutes

12 Sant'Erasmo castraure baby artichokes (or any baby artichokes)
2 spider or swimmer crabs (or any hard-shelled crabs)
14 oz (400 g) clams (soaked overnight in cold salted water), mussels, or razor clams
14 oz (400 g) raw large shrimp, unpeeled
4 scampi/langoustines (or large shrimp)
1 cup (7 oz/200 g) fresh mixed herbs (chervil, parsley, oregano, micro basil, micro chard)
Scant ½ cup (100 ml) Isola delle Rose extra virgin olive oil (or any quality extra virgin olive oil)
1 lemon, cut in half
Sea salt and freshly ground black pepper

This is another beautiful, simple dish that relies totally on the quality and freshness of its ingredients. Italians call dishes like this salads, even though they're made almost entirely of seafood and—as in this instance—include only baby artichokes as the vegetable. Feel free to use any sort of seafood or fish here, just make sure it's high quality. Do the same with the olive oil. The one I've used is a product from an absolutely stunning Venetian island called Isola delle Rose, which was built during the Fascist era and now boasts an amazing resort as well as a 100-year-old olive grove.

To cook the artichokes, simply put them whole in a pan of cold salted water and bring to a boil. Simmer for 10–20 minutes or until just cooked through to the center (you can check this with a skewer).

Once the artichokes are cooked, remove from the water and leave to cool; gently remove the outer leaves until you reach leaves that are tender enough to eat. Trim the base of each artichoke, removing the fibrous exterior. Set aside until ready to use (they are served whole).

Prepare the crabs by removing the outer shells and then the feathery gills. Wash and cut the crabs in half.

Drain the clams, if using. Prepare the mussels by removing the beards and cleaning the shells. Prepare the razor clams by cleaning the shells.

Devein the shrimp and scampi by using a toothpick to pierce the back of the head to a depth of a few millimeters, then lift up the end of the toothpick to scoop out the alimentary vein. Pull the vein gently to remove.

Next, using a large steamer or steaming oven, steam the shellfish for 5–10 minutes or until cooked. All the mussels and clams should have opened. All the shellfish should take about the same time to cook, unless there are large variations in size.

Once cooked, remove the shellfish and place the baby artichokes into the steamer to heat for 1–2 minutes.

In a small bowl, season the herbs with sea salt and pepper, drizzle with the extra virgin olive oil, and mix together.

Serve everything warm on a big platter with the lemon halves and scattered with herbs. The scampi and shrimp can be served whole or cut in half, and either completely or partially peeled. Serve with finger bowls.

—Serves 4

ROASTED VENETIAN DUCK AND PRUNES
with POTATO AND ZUCCHINI TORTA

Prep Time 25 minutes, plus 2 hours for prunes to steep
Cooking Time 1 hour 30 minutes

1½ cups (10½ oz/300 g) pitted
  prunes
⅔ cup (3½ oz/100 g) pistachios
1 deboned whole duck, skin
  on but excess fat removed
¾ cup (180 ml) red wine
3 tablespoons orange juice
¼ cup (1¾ oz/50 g) sugar
2 cloves
4 black peppercorns
1 cinnamon stick
1 lb 2 oz (500 g) ground pork
  (30% fat)
3 garlic cloves, chopped
½ cup (1 oz/30 g) chopped parsley
2 tablespoons olive oil
Sea salt and freshly ground
  black pepper

Potato and zucchini torta
1 lb 5 oz (600 g) potatoes
10½ oz (300 g) zucchini
5 tablespoons (2½ oz/70 g) butter,
  melted
2 cups (7 oz/200 g) grated
  Parmigiano Reggiano

Duck is one of the few stalwarts of Venetian cooking that isn't centered around fish or seafood. It is historically a regal protein, as fish was considered "common" food for much of Venice's history. Wild duck was generally used before farmed products became available, delivering a much leaner protein. Fat (and therefore flavor) was incorporated via a process of larding—literally wrapping the duck in lardo. This recipe, albeit without the indulgent lardo, is an absolute classic, but be warned, it hinges on two things: the fat content of the pork (make sure it's 30 percent) as well as the cooking time. Keep your eye on both and you'll enjoy a stunningly succulent and tender result. Wild duck can be used if you can find it, but I'd suggest larding to ensure the retention of moisture.

Cut the prunes into quarters and place in a heat-resistant bowl. Pour the red wine mixture over the top and let steep for at least 2 hours.

Preheat the oven to 325°F (170°C). Arrange the pistachios evenly on a baking sheet and cook for 6–8 minutes, or until lightly browned. Remove from the oven and transfer the nuts to a plate to prevent them from over-coloring. Allow to cool completely.

Place the deboned duck on a baking sheet, season with salt and pepper on both sides, and refrigerate.

In a medium-sized saucepan, bring the red wine, orange juice, sugar, cloves, peppercorns, and cinnamon to a boil. Turn down the heat and simmer for 15 minutes.

Preheat the oven to 350°F (180°C).

Remove half the prunes from the wine marinade and combine with the ground pork, pistachios, garlic, and parsley. Season with salt and pepper. Roll the stuffing into a thick log, approximately the same length as the duck.

Remove the deboned duck from the refrigerator and place skin-side down on a work surface, then spread open. Place the stuffing lengthways into the middle of the duck. Fold the sides over to form a cylindrical shape, tuck the ends under, and, using cooking twine, tie at even intervals along the duck.

Brush the duck with the olive oil and place on a rack in a roasting pan. Roast for about 1 hour or until golden and crisp, basting every 15 minutes with its own fat.

Meanwhile, to make the potato and zucchini torta, slice the potatoes and zucchini as thinly as possible, then toss with the butter and season with salt and pepper. In a medium-sized baking dish, layer the potato and zucchini alternately, sprinkling a little cheese between each layer. Finish with a layer of Parmigiano.

When the duck has been in the oven for 30 minutes, add the torta and bake for 40 minutes or until golden in color.

Meanwhile, heat the remaining prunes and red wine marinade in a saucepan over low heat.

When cooked, remove the duck from the oven and cover with foil. Rest for about 10 minutes while the torta finishes cooking.

Remove the string from the duck and slice into portions. Serve with the potato and zucchini torta, the remaining prunes, and the warm marinade as a sauce.

Note
Deboned duck can be found in good supermarkets, gourmet food stores, or specialty butchers.

—Serves 6

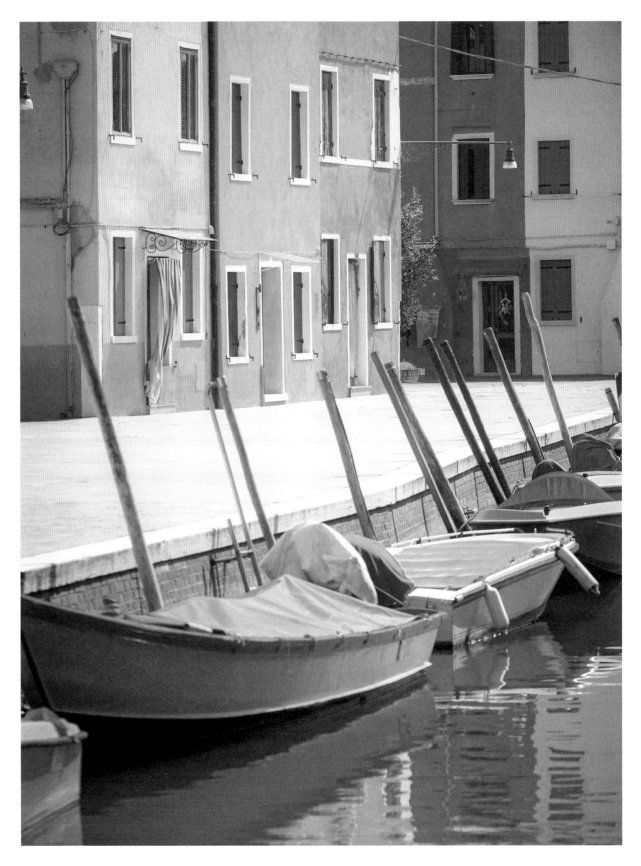

ROASTED JOHN DORY
with PORCINI MUSHROOMS AND CRISP POTATOES

Prep Time 30 minutes
Cooking Time 20 minutes

½ lemon
1 lb 12 oz (800 g) John Dory, cleaned, scaled, and deboned
½ cup (¼ oz/8 g) thyme sprigs
10½ oz (300 g) potatoes
Generous ¾ cup (200 ml) Lake Garda extra virgin olive oil (or any quality early-harvest extra virgin olive oil)
4 garlic cloves, sliced
7 oz (200 g) fresh or frozen porcini mushrooms (or king brown mushrooms)
Sea salt and freshly ground black pepper

For me, porcini are the king of all mushrooms. I share this opinion with a lot of people, who find the flavor and texture of porcini equally amazing. Of course, porcini are particularly enjoyable fresh, but don't be reluctant to use a quality fresh-frozen product if they are unavailable—they can be difficult to source fresh, especially outside Europe. While porcini and fish is not a common pairing, the combination is fantastic.

Cut the lemon into slices and place inside the belly cavity of the John Dory with the fresh thyme. Season with salt and pepper, inside and out.

Peel, then finely slice the potatoes into ⅛ inch (3 mm) rounds and toss with generous ½ cup (150 ml) extra virgin olive oil and the sliced garlic. Season with salt and pepper.

Spread the sliced potatoes and garlic evenly on a large baking sheet. Place the John Dory on top of the potatoes.

Slice the porcini mushrooms into ¼ inch (5 mm) pieces and scatter over the John Dory. Drizzle with the remaining oil.

Preheat the oven to 350°F (180°C). Place the baking sheet in the oven and cook for 20 minutes.

Serve the fish on a serving platter with the juices from the baking sheet, porcini mushrooms, and crisp potatoes.

—Serves 2

SEARED CHICKEN LIVERS *with* MUSCATEL GRAPES, SOUR CHERRIES, AND BIANCOPERLA WHITE POLENTA

Prep Time 15 minutes
Cooking Time 40 minutes

2½ cups (600 ml) Chicken
   Stock (page 236)
½ cup (3½ oz/100 g) Biancoperla
   white polenta (or any coarse
   white polenta cornmeal)
4 tablespoons grated
   Parmigiano Reggiano
1 lb 5 oz (600 g) chicken livers
2 tablespoons extra virgin olive
   oil, plus extra for brushing
   the polenta
2 tablespoons (1 oz/30 g) butter
5½ oz (160 g) candied
   sour cherries, drained
   (or any cherries in syrup)
5½ oz (160 g) fresh
   Muscatel grapes
Sea salt and freshly ground
   black pepper

Despite the dominance of seafood across Venice and her islands, the archipelago is also very well known for its delicious handling of liver. The most iconic traditional dish is *fegato alla Venezia*—calf livers with onion—famous throughout the whole of the Veneto, if not the entire country. While not as common as their veal counterparts, chicken and duck livers are also enjoyed throughout Venice. Regardless of the type of liver you're working with, make sure you handle it with care. There's nothing worse than overcooked liver—all it needs is a quick flash in the pan to create a lovely creamy and tender texture.

In a large saucepan, bring 2 cups (500 ml) of the stock to a boil, then slowly pour in the polenta in a steady stream, stirring continuously. Cook for 30 minutes over low heat, then add the Parmigiano and season with salt and pepper.

Pour the cooked polenta into a baking dish. When it is cold, cut it into 2½ inch (6 cm) squares.

Using a sharp knife, remove any connective tissue from the livers, then wash under cold water and pat dry with a paper towels.

Heat a large sauté pan over high heat for 1 minute. Add the olive oil to the pan and heat until it begins to smoke. Season the livers with salt and pepper, place in the pan, and quickly brown on all sides, then transfer to a plate and set aside somewhere warm.

Turn the heat down to low, add 1 tablespoon butter to the pan, and cook until nutty-brown. Add the cherries and grapes and turn the heat to high. Add the remaining chicken stock and cook until reduced by half. Stir in the remaining butter.

Preheat the broiler, then brush the polenta with olive oil and broil for 2 minutes on each side.

Serve the polenta immediately with the livers, grapes, and sour cherries.

—Serves 4

Dolci

CARROT, HAZELNUT, AND SPELT CAKE *with* HAZELNUT GELATO

Prep Time 20 minutes, plus resting the frosting, and churning and freezing the gelato
Cooking Time 45 minutes

Hazelnut gelato
2¾ cups (670 ml) milk
¾ cup (5 oz/140 g) sugar
¼ cup (1 oz/30 g) powdered
    skim milk
6 tablespoons (2 oz/60 g)
    dextrose
Scant ½ cup (3½ oz/100 g)
    hazelnut paste

Chocolate frosting
7 oz (200 g) 70% dark chocolate
Generous ¾ cup (200 ml) heavy
    cream

Carrot, hazelnut, and spelt cake
5 eggs, separated
1 pinch salt
1 cup (8 oz/225 g) sugar
3 tablespoons hot water
3¾ cups (14½ oz/410 g) grated
    carrots
3 cups (10½ oz/295 g) ground
    hazelnuts
½ cup (2 oz/60 g) spelt flour
½ teaspoon baking powder
½ teaspoon ground cinnamon
1 tablespoon rum
1 teaspoon vanilla bean paste

The land-based town of Chioggia, commonly referred to as "Little Venice," has been very important to Venice throughout history. It supplies her with super-premium, fresh seafood (it boasts Italy's largest retail and wholesale fish market) as well as a wide array of fruit and vegetables, including its highly sought-after carrots.

To make the hazelnut gelato, half fill the base pan of a double boiler with water and bring to a simmer. Place the milk in the double boiler over medium heat.

Measuring with a candy thermometer, when the milk reaches 104°F (40°C) add the rest of the ingredients to the milk then wait for the temperature to reach 149°F (65°C). Continue cooking for 30 minutes at 149°F (65°C), stirring regularly. Blend the mixture with an immersion blender, then churn in an ice cream machine to 25°F (-4°C).

Meanwhile, make the chocolate frosting. Place the chocolate in a heat-resistant bowl. Bring the cream to a simmer in a pan over low heat. Pour the cream over the chocolate and leave to stand for 30 seconds, then stir through. Cover with plastic wrap and leave at room temperature for 2 hours.

Preheat the oven to 315°F (160°C).

Whisk the egg whites and salt in a stainless steel bowl until light and fluffy soft peaks form. Slowly add ⅓ cup (2½ oz/75 g) of the sugar, increasing the speed to high until stiff peaks form.

In another bowl, beat the egg yolks and hot water with an electric mixer on medium speed until light and foamy. Slowly add the remaining sugar and then beat on high for 3 minutes until pale and thick.

In a third bowl, combine the carrots, ground hazelnuts, spelt flour, baking powder, ground cinnamon, rum, and vanilla bean paste.

Fold the egg whites into the whipped egg yolks until combined, then fold into the carrot mixture in two batches.

Grease a 10 inch (25 cm) springform cake pan and pour in the batter. Bake for 50 minutes.

Remove from the cake from the oven and cool on a cake rack. Using a spatula, spread the chocolate frosting evenly over the cake.

Note
Dextrose and hazelnut paste can be bought online and at specialty stores.

—*Serves 8*

GRILLED WHITE PEACHES *with* WHITE WINE GRANITA *and* FIOR DI LATTE GELATO

Prep Time 15 minutes, plus granita and gelato freezing
Cooking Time 50 minutes

4 ripe white peaches
1 tablespoon olive oil

White wine granita
¼ cup (2 oz/60 g) sugar
6 white peaches, pitted and quartered
½ cup (125 ml) Cavazza Durello sparkling white wine (or any quality sparkling wine)

Fior di latte gelato
2¾ cups (650 ml) milk
½ cup (120 ml) light cream
¾ cup (5 oz/140 g) sugar
½ cup (1½ oz/40 g) powdered skim milk
3 tablespoons (1¼ oz/35 g) dextrose

During summer, white peaches are abundant throughout the Veneto and Venice. This recipe is all about showcasing this delightful stone fruit, so make a point of finding peaches that are at their peak of ripeness, and therefore beautifully sweet. They are fantastic with the granita, which showcases an exceptional sparkling wine called Durello, produced in the hills that border Verona and Vicenza, in an area called Monti Lessini. While any quality sparkling wine can be used here, the Durello boasts great structure and acidity, with a lovely aroma of honey and orchard fruit.

To make the granita, place the sugar and ½ cup (125 ml) water in a small saucepan over low heat and cook until the sugar dissolves and becomes a syrup.

Extract the juice from the peach quarters using an electric juicer (or process to a pulp and squeeze through a fine mesh strainer). You will need 3 cups (750 ml) juice. Stir the peach juice and wine into the sugar syrup.

Pour this granita mixture into a shallow dish and freeze for 2 hours. Just before serving, use a fork to scrape the frozen granita into crystals.

To make the gelato, half-fill the base pan of a double boiler with water and bring to a simmer. Place the milk and cream in the double boiler over medium heat, stirring constantly, and bring to 104°F (40°C) on a candy thermometer.

Combine the sugar, powdered milk, and dextrose, and stir into the milk mixture. Stir every 5 minutes for 30 minutes, or until the temperature reaches 149°F (65°C).

Transfer the gelato mixture to a stainless steel bowl over ice and bring the temperature down to 104°F (40°C). Place in the freezer and stir every 10 minutes until the temperature reaches 39°F (4°C).

Place the mixture in an ice cream machine and churn to 25°F (-4°C).

Preheat a grill or grill pan until medium-hot. Halve the 4 peaches and remove the pits. Lightly brush the cut sides with olive oil. Place the peaches cut-side down on the grill or pan and cook for 4 minutes, then turn over and grill again for 2 minutes or until softened.

Serve the grilled peaches with the granita and gelato.

Notes
Dextrose can be bought online and at specialty stores.

This recipe makes more granita and gelato than is needed here, so store the remainder in separate containers in the freezer and enjoy with fresh berries. The granita can be used as a mixer with prosecco.

—Serves 4

OSTERIA ALLE TESTIERE PISTACHIO CAKE
with PISTACHIO GELATO

Prep Time 15 minutes, plus overnight gelato cooling, churning, and freezing
Cooking Time 1 hour 30 minutes

Pistachio cake
2½ cups (10½ oz/300 g)
    pistachios, skin on
6 eggs
1¼ cups (9 oz/250 g) sugar
10½ tablespoons (5½ oz/150 g)
    butter, softened
½ cup (3½ oz/100 g) potato starch
1 teaspoon baking powder
Confectioners' sugar,
    for dusting

Pistachio gelato
2 cups (500 ml) milk
5 egg yolks
3 tablespoons (2 oz/60 g)
    honey
¾ cup (5½ oz/150 g) sugar
¾ cup (3½ oz/100 g) pistachios,
    peeled
Generous ½ cup (150 ml) light
    cream
2 tablespoons pure pistachio
    paste

Every time I'm in Venice I visit one of my favorite trattorias, Osteria alle Testiere, which serves some of the freshest, most incredible seafood I've ever had the pleasure of eating. But that's never the sole reason for my visit: Testiere's desserts are some of the very best in Venice, and none more so than their pistachio cake. It is absolute heaven and beautiful in its simplicity. It's imperative to source the highest quality ingredients, particularly the pistachios, which give the cake its lovely green color and lightness.

To make the pistachio gelato, bring the milk to a simmer in a pan over low heat. Whisk the egg yolks, honey, and sugar until thick and creamy in an ovensafe bowl. Pour the milk over the egg mixture and stir until combined.

Place the ovensafe bowl over a pan of simmering water and, stirring regularly, bring to 185°F (85°C) on a candy thermometer. This should take 15–20 minutes. The mixture should coat the back of a spoon. Pass the mixture through a fine sieve into a clean container and chill overnight in the fridge.

Grind the pistachios in a food processor to make a fine meal. Lightly whip the cream and fold in the pistachios and pistachio paste.

Place the chilled mixture in a gelato machine and churn until just set, then add the cream and pistachio mix and churn again for 2 minutes. Transfer the gelato into a plastic or metal container and store in the freezer until ready to use.

Preheat the oven to 315°F (160°C).

To make the pistachio cake, grind the pistachios in a food processor to make a fine meal.

Beat the eggs with the sugar. Beat in the butter. Sift the potato flour starch with the baking powder and add to the mixture gently. Finally, stir in the pistachio meal a little at a time.

Pour the mixture into a greased and lined 10 inch (26 cm) round cake pan and bake for 55–60 minutes. Test by inserting a skewer into the middle of the cake: if it comes out clean, the cake is done. Allow the cake to cool, then remove from the pan.

Once completely cool, dust the cake with confectioners' sugar, slice, and serve with a scoop of the gelato.

Note
Pistachio paste can be bought online and at specialty stores.

—Serves 8

VENETIAN CREMA ROSADA

Prep Time 10 minutes, plus setting and chilling
Cooking Time 1 hour

Generous 1 cup (3½ oz/100 g)
    sliced almonds
¾ cup (4 oz/120 g) raisins
Rum, for soaking the raisins
12 eggs
¾ cup (5½ oz/150 g) sugar
2½ cups (600 ml) milk
2½ cups (600 ml) light cream
4 teaspoons Rosolio liqueur
    (or any preferred liqueur
    or rum)
½ cup (3½ oz/100 g) maraschino
    cherries

This Venetian crème caramel, or *crema rosada*, is found throughout the Veneto, in Venice, along the Dalmatian coast, and is even quite famous in Dubrovnik. Its name refers to Rosolio, the rose-scented liqueur used in the traditional recipe, but far less prevalent today. Despite the fact that nowadays people use a wide range of liqueurs or spirits—most commonly rum—the rose-inspired name has stuck.

Preheat the oven to 325°F (170°C). Arrange the almonds evenly on a baking sheet and roast for 8–10 minutes, or until golden brown. Remove from the oven and transfer to a plate to prevent them from over-coloring. Allow to cool completely before using.

Reduce the oven temperature to 300°F (150°C).

Put the raisins in a bowl with enough rum to just cover them. Set aside to soak.

In a large bowl, mix the eggs with 2 tablespoons of the sugar until a pale cream color. Add the milk, cream, and liqueur and combine with a spatula.

Place the remaining sugar in a small saucepan and cook, without stirring, over low heat for 3–5 minutes until a deep caramel color. Pour the caramel into an ovensafe glass bowl, 9 inches (23 cm) in diameter and 4 inches (10 cm) deep, covering the base evenly. Leave to set in a cool place.

Pour the cream mix into the bowl, making sure it is evenly distributed. Place the bowl in a deep roasting pan and pour hot water into the pan until it reaches three-quarters of the way up the side of the bowl.

Bake in the oven for 45 minutes: it should still wobble in the center when gently shaken. Remove from the pan and refrigerate until completely chilled.

Run a small knife around the edge of the bowl, then turn out the *crema rosada* onto a serving plate. Serve with the rum-soaked raisins, maraschino cherries, and toasted almonds.

—*Serves 10*

THE VENETO

II

THE LAND-BASED MARKETPLACE OF AN AQUATIC EMPIRE

With its diverse landscape and highly desirable arable land, the Veneto was the land-based jewel in the Venetian Republic's otherwise water-based crown. Today it is a treasure trove of some of Italy's finest food and wine products.

As one-third of the historical region of the Triveneto (Veneto, Friuli Venezia Giulia, and Trentino Alto Adige), Veneto was a key piece of the trading puzzle for Venice. Waverley Root makes the point eloquently:

Venice needed her hinterland not only as a market for the goods she imported from the East, but also as a supplier of staple foods like wheat, which could not be raised on her small islands; this freed her from dependence on foodstuffs brought in by sea, and made her invulnerable to blockade.

It's easy to see how this flourishing agricultural hinterland came to form an integral cog in the wheel of the Venetian Republic. Water, however, was key again to the Republic's success on land. As has been reiterated through the ages, the Venetians were at their best on water. In order to access and take full advantage of the fruits of the Veneto, the Republic built and fortified canals and manipulated existing waterways to facilitate trade. After all, water was by far the quickest way to get around at the time—even across the land.

And, despite the Veneto region's rich resources and sheer size, she was completely dominated by Venice. What the Veneto had in agricultural prowess and natural resources, it lacked in wealth and entrepreneurialism. Venice had these in spades, and distinctively imbued her culture on the region. This is no more evident than in the cuisine of the Veneto where, unlike in any other land-based region of

Italy, seafood plays a uniquely fundamental role. This is thanks solely to Venice's influence. The Po river, Lake Garda, the Venetian lagoon, and the other waterways of the Veneto were, and continue to be, a rich source of fish and game meat, which have always been preferred over more land-based proteins.

Take Padua, for instance, where many of the specialties in the city, some 25 miles (40 km) from the sea, are local variants of Venetian dishes, or can be linked back directly to the Republic's trading era. Once again, seafood is prominent. *Scampi alla busara* is a popular dish, as are Venetian staples such as lagoon octopus, sardines *in saor*, fried school shrimp, and cuttlefish: boiled or cooked in its own ink.

Padua is even brave enough to claim herself as the real birthplace of *risi e bisi*, not a seafood dish, but one of Venice's most iconic menu items, comprising rice and (in its truest form) Veneto peas.

Moving northwest to Vicenza, which the Republic took hold of in the early 1400s, Venice's impact is impossible to avoid. Vicenza embraced Venice's culture and customs—even to the point where it was referred to as "Venice on dry land." Despite its inland location, Vicenza—like Venice—prefers seafood, poultry, and game to the usual quadruped meats of pork, veal, and beef. Its signature dish, *baccala alla vicentina*, is another treatment of the classically Venetian staple, salt cod.

Almost one-third of Veneto's surface is mountainous, and it is these regions that produce the unique artisanal cheeses, charcuterie, and meats that the Veneto and Venetian people eat. The plain of the Po Valley covers more than half of the region, extending from the mountains on the Austrian border to the Adriatic, and is home to some of the Republic's most valuable commodities, namely rice and maize, from which risotto and polenta—the heart and soul of Venetian cooking—are made.

As ubiquitous as rice and polenta are in this region, so too are the various forms of the Veneto's favorite vegetable: radicchio. There are a number of different varieties, and they're treated in a plethora of different ways, both in the Veneto and her capital, Venice: grilled, roasted, braised, fried, eaten raw, tossed in salads, and cooked in risottos. Where other prime agricultural areas in Italy usually offer tourists wine trails, the Veneto has an equivalent—for radicchio.

And wine is key here too, for the Veneto has historically provided the liquid fuel of Venetian society. The Veneto—where viticulture is said to have been established in the Bronze Age—is home to some of Italy's most iconic wine-producing regions, including the Valpolicella, Soave, and Valdobbiadene, and contains a selection of some of Italy's most esteemed producers. We feature some of these in the following pages.

Grappa is also very important in the Veneto region where—perhaps more than anywhere else in Italy—almost every meal is sealed with a nip of grappa (breakfast coffee also often involves this ubiquitous spirit—particularly during the cold of winter).

While it's absolutely true that seafood plays a key role in the diet of Veneto people, by virtue of the region's geography it's also true that vegetable and meat-based dishes are more common here than anywhere else in the Republic. It's for this reason that this chapter focuses on the more land-based wonders of this historical agricultural territory and marketplace.

THE VENETO

Antipasti

OLIVE-OIL FRIED SCHOOL SHRIMP
with CRISPY HERBS *and* BIANCOPERLA WHITE POLENTA

Prep Time 15 minutes
Cooking Time 55 minutes

⅔ cup (4½ oz/130 g) Biancoperla
    white polenta (or any coarse
    white polenta cornmeal)
7 tablespoons (3½ oz/100 g)
    butter
Olive oil, for deep-frying
1 lb 2 oz (500 g) *schie*
    (school shrimp or bay shrimp),
    whole and unpeeled
All-purpose flour, for dusting
2 handfuls mixed herbs
    (Italian parsley, sage, marjoram)
Sea salt and freshly ground
    black pepper

In and around the lagoon, *schie* (known to many as school shrimp) are really, really small. They're just delightful, and this dish is an absolute crowd-pleaser. If you're not able to find *schie*, any baby or school shrimp will create delicious results—just try to keep them bite-sized. Eat them whole and enjoy the crunch!

To make the polenta, bring 3¼ cups (800 ml) salted water to a boil in a large pot. Add the polenta slowly in a constant stream, stirring continuously.

Turn the heat down to low and cook for 45 minutes, stirring regularly. Add the butter to the polenta and adjust the seasoning to taste.

Heat the olive oil to 350°F (180°C) in a deep fryer or a deep pan.

Toss the shrimp in the flour and shake off any excess. Add the shrimp to the hot oil, fry for 3 minutes until crisp, and then drain on paper towels and season with salt and pepper.

Using the same pan, fry the herbs, in batches, for about 30 seconds per batch or until crisp. Drain on paper towels.

Serve the fried shrimp on the polenta, garnished with the fried herbs.

—Serves 4

THE VENETO ✳ *Antipasti*

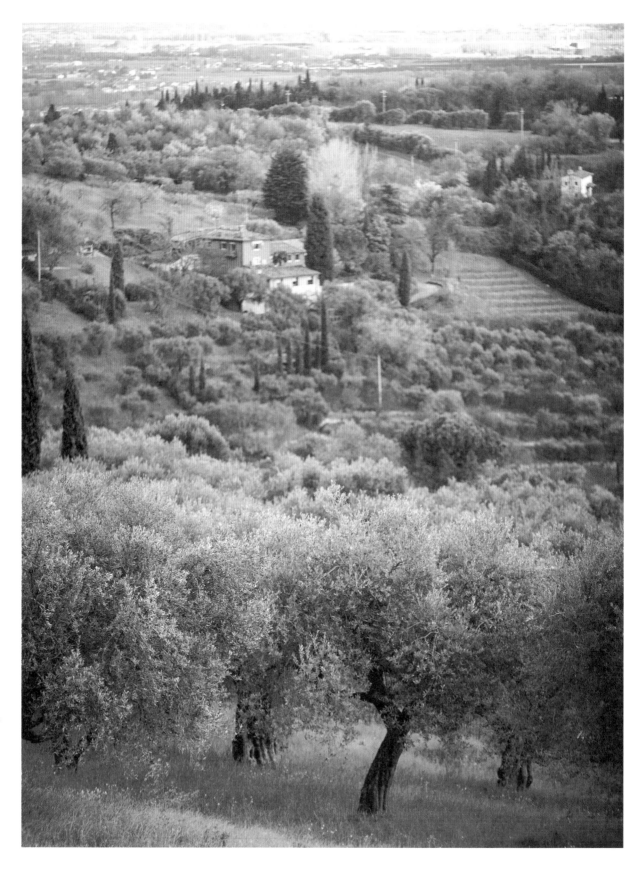

BASSANO WHITE ASPARAGUS
with MOUNTAIN HEN EGG SALAD

Prep Time 10 minutes, plus 2 days for soaking the radicchio
Cooking Time 20 minutes

1 handful mixed radicchio
    and Belgian endive
16 spears Bassano del Grappa
    white asparagus (or any white
    or green asparagus)
4 tablespoons sea salt, plus
    extra to taste
8 mountain hen eggs (or any large
    free-range chicken or duck
    eggs)
1 handful mixed herbs
    (Italian parsley, oregano, basil)
4 tablespoons Lake Garda
    extra virgin olive oil (or any
    quality early-harvest extra
    virgin olive oil)
Shaved or grated Parmigiano
    Reggiano, to serve (optional)

Valpolicella vinaigrette
1 garlic clove
Scant ½ cup (100 ml) Valpolicella
    red wine vinegar (or any
    quality red wine vinegar)
1⅔ cups (400 ml) Lake Garda
    extra virgin olive oil (or any
    quality early-harvest extra
    virgin olive oil)
Sea salt and freshly ground
    black pepper

White asparagus is an absolutely stunning product of the Veneto region, and is available around the world at different times of the year. The flavor profile is different to green asparagus—it isn't as herbaceous—but this recipe is beautiful with either. It's a lovely, simple dish that lets the quality of the ingredients speak for themselves; perfect for late winter or spring.

Soak the radicchio in a bowl of cold water in the fridge for 2 days, changing the water three to four times. Drain, then set aside.

Using a sharp knife, prepare the asparagus by cutting the woody bottom off each spear. You can test how far the woody section goes by bending the end of one spear and seeing where it breaks. Alternatively, the woody ends can be peeled.

Fill a large deep pot with water, add the salt, and bring to a rapid boil. Place the asparagus in the boiling water and cook for 5–8 minutes, or until just becoming tender: this will depend on the size and density of the asparagus. Remove the asparagus from the water and set aside.

Fill a saucepan with water and bring to a boil, add the eggs, and cook for 6 minutes. Remove and peel when cool enough to handle.

To make the vinaigrette, crush the garlic with the side of a knife and rub it around the inside of a mixing bowl. Add the red wine vinegar, then slowly whisk in the extra virgin olive oil. Season to taste.

Pick the leaves from the mixed herbs, discarding the stalks. Toss the radicchio and herbs with 4 tablespoons of the Valpolicella vinaigrette and season with a pinch of sea salt. Arrange the salad on individual serving plates.

Add 4 asparagus spears to each plate. Break the eggs onto the asparagus, letting the yolks run over the salad. Drizzle with the extra virgin olive oil and season with salt and black pepper. This salad is also wonderful with shaved or grated Parmigiano Reggiano.

Note
Radicchio is renowned for being quite a bitter leaf, so we soak it in water beforehand for a sweeter flavor. In Italy a great deal of radicchio is eaten, and the most bitter types are treated in a similar way before sale. Consequently, most radicchio sold in Italy is less bitter than in other places around the world.

—Serves 4

THE VENETO ✳ *Antipasti*

TRUFFLED VERONESE BOGONI SNAILS

Prep Time 20 minutes
Cooking Time 20 minutes

24 large European snails
2 tablespoons extra virgin olive oil
2 tablespoons finely chopped
French shallots
2 tablespoons finely
chopped celery
4 tablespoons finely chopped
frozen/fresh porcini or
fresh portobello mushrooms
2 garlic cloves, minced
1 teaspoon chopped thyme
½ cup (125 ml) Garganega white
wine (or any quality dry
white wine)
1 tablespoon chopped parsley
3 sticks (13 oz/360 g) butter,
softened
¾ oz (20 g) black truffle, finely
grated
4 teaspoons fresh breadcrumbs
Sea salt and freshly ground
black pepper

This dish comes from a beautiful part of the Veneto called the Euganean Hills, famous for its abundance of produce, including local truffles. The very earthy ingredients in this dish—the mushrooms and truffles particularly— are, for me, the taste of the Veneto, and a fundamental agricultural asset during the Venetian Republic's reign. In this region, and across Italy more broadly, snails—usually synonymous with French cooking—have been enjoyed on a very regular basis and in a multitude of different ways over the years. This is just one of many, and a personal favorite.

Preheat the oven to 350°F (180°C).

Place the snails in a sink of cold water and wash, rubbing between your hands to remove any dirt from the shells. Drain and repeat the washing process.

Bring a large pot of water to a boil. Place the snails in the boiling water and cook for 3 minutes, discarding any snails that float. Drain and let cool. Remove meat from the shells with a small pick, reserving the shells.

Heat a frying pan over low heat. Add the olive oil, shallots, celery, mushrooms, garlic, and thyme and cook for 5 minutes, stirring regularly. Add the white wine and cook until reduced by half.

Add the snails and parsley. Season to taste. Remove from the heat and allow to cool.

Mix the softened butter with the black truffle and season with sea salt. Add half the truffle butter and half the breadcrumbs to the snail mix.

Place the mushroom and snail mix back into the shells, being sure to include one snail per shell. Seal the top of the shells with the remaining truffle butter and sprinkle with the remaining breadcrumbs.

Place the snails on an ovensafe snail platter or on a baking sheet lined with coarse salt so that the snails stay upright. Bake for 8–10 minutes.

Notes
In many places outside Europe, several ingredients for this recipe might be difficult to source. If fresh porcini mushrooms are unavailable, any fresh wild European mushrooms can be substituted.

If fresh snails are difficult to obtain, quality flash-frozen snails may be substituted and can be found in gourmet food stores.

This recipe makes more truffle butter than is needed here. You can freeze the remainder and use it tossed through fresh pasta or risotto, or to season steamed vegetables or roasted or grilled fish or meat.

—*Serves 4*

THE VENETO ✳ *Antipasti*

GRILLED SOPRESSA SALAMI *with* RED CORN POLENTA *and* TREVISO "IN SAOR"

Prep Time 20 minutes, plus 2 days for soaking and 2 hours for marinating the radicchio
Cooking Time 1 hour

1 Treviso radicchio, quartered (or any radicchio)
Generous ½ cup (3 oz/80 g) pine nuts
Generous ½ cup (150 ml) extra virgin olive oil
2 white onions, sliced
3 bay leaves
½ cup (3 oz/85 g) raisins
5 black peppercorns
5 tablespoons red wine vinegar
3 tablespoons sugar
½ tablespoon salt, for blanching
White wine vinegar, for blanching
2 cups (500 ml) Chicken Stock (page 236)
½ cup (3½ oz/95 g) coarse red corn (Storo) polenta (or yellow or white polenta cornmeal)
4 tablespoons finely grated Parmigiano Reggiano
2 tablespoons (1 oz/30 g) butter
14 oz (400 g) Sopressa Veneta salami (or any fresh high fat-content salami)
Sea salt

In saor is a classic Venetian marinade, borne out of necessity rather than creativity. Traditionally used for fish—predominantly sardines—the vinegar would preserve the Venetian fishermen's meals in a time well before the luxury of refrigeration. Today, the sweet-and-sour sauce is a classic component of a number of dishes in and around Venice and the Veneto, typically combining vinegar with raisins, pine nuts, and onions. While it is most commonly partnered with seafood, it can also be used with vegetables, such as the radicchio I've chosen here.

Soak the radicchio in a bowl of cold water in the fridge for 2 days, changing the water three or four times. Drain.

Preheat the oven to 325°F (170°C). Arrange the pine nuts evenly on a baking sheet and roast for 6–8 minutes, or until lightly browned. Remove from the oven and transfer to a plate to prevent them from over-coloring.

Heat the olive oil in a saucepan over medium heat, add the onion and bay leaves, and cook for 5 minutes until tender. Add the raisins, black peppercorns, red wine vinegar, and sugar and simmer for 5 minutes. This is your *saor* mixture.

To prepare the radicchio, blanch for 5 minutes in a mixture of boiling salted water and white wine vinegar (we use a ratio of roughly three times water to vinegar). Drain, pat dry with paper towels, and put in a small bowl. Pour the *saor* mixture over the radicchio and leave to marinate for 2 hours.

Bring the chicken stock to a simmer in a pot. Season with salt and slowly pour in the polenta. Cook for 45 minutes over low heat, stirring continuously.

Add the Parmigiano and mix through. Add the butter, mix vigorously, and adjust the seasoning, adding more salt if needed.

Cut the salami into ¼ inch (5 mm) slices. Preheat a griddle or frying pan, add a little oil, and fry the salami for 1–2 minutes on each side.

To serve, place the polenta on serving plates, top with the salami, and garnish with the radicchio *in saor* and toasted pine nuts.

Notes
Radicchio is renowned for being quite a bitter leaf, so for a sweeter flavor soak the radicchio in water before using, as detailed above.

The key to getting this recipe just right is sourcing a high-fat salami that's fresh and moist. We've used Sopressa Veneta salami, but any high-quality, high-fat salami can be substituted.

—*Serves 4*

Pasta, rice, and pies

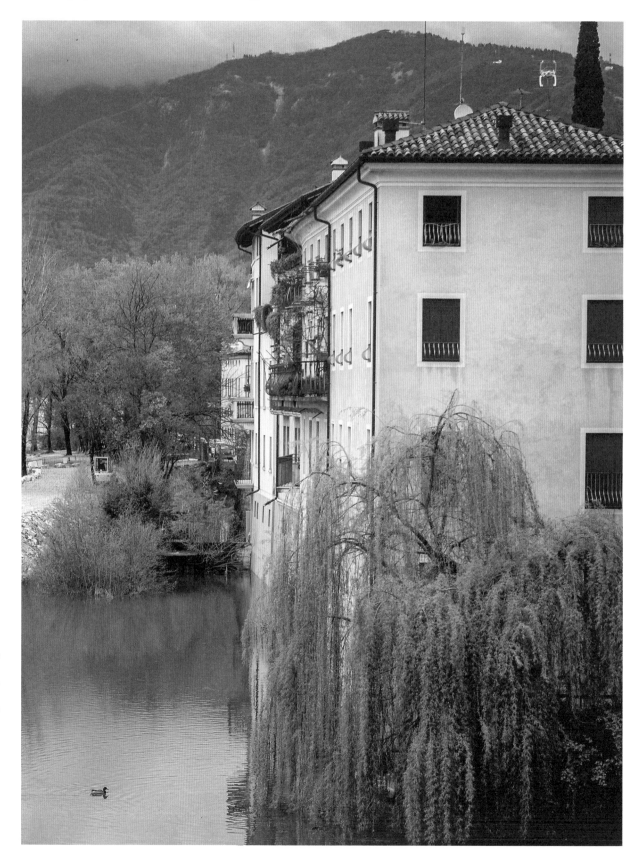

THE VENETO ✳ *Pasta, rice, and pies*

BASSANO RADICCHIO, VESPAIOLO, AND STRACCHINO RISOTTO

Prep Time 15 minutes, plus 2 days for soaking the radicchio
Cooking Time 30 minutes

2 oz (60 g) radicchio, chopped
  into ½ inch (1 cm) squares
Scant ¼ cup (50 ml) olive oil
3 French shallots, finely diced
1 garlic clove, finely sliced
1¾ cups (12½ oz/350 g) Vialone
  Nano rice (or any risotto rice)
Generous ¾ cup (200 ml)
  Vespaiolo white wine
  (or any good dry white wine)
3⅓ cups (800 ml) Chicken or
  Vegetable Stock (pages 236–7)
7 oz (200 g) Stracchino cheese
  (Morlacco cheese should
  be used if available)
Grated Parmigiano Reggiano,
  to serve (optional)
Sea salt and freshly ground
  black pepper

This recipe is traditionally made with a very typical local wine, Vespaiolo, as well as another gorgeous local product, Morlacco—Stracchino cheese that has been aged for between 20 days and 3 months. This dish is beautiful with Stracchino, but is taken to another level with the aged cheese. Morlacco is rarely found outside Italy, but give it your best shot at your gourmet deli or specialty food store.

Soak the radicchio in a bowl of cold water in the fridge for 2 days, changing the water three or four times. Drain, then blanch the radicchio for 5 minutes in a pot of lightly salted water. Drain and set aside.

Heat the olive oil in a heavy-bottomed pan over low heat for 1 minute. Add the French shallots and garlic and cook for 3 minutes, stirring continuously.

Add the rice and cook, stirring, until the rice is translucent and fully coated with oil. Stir in the white wine and cook for 2 minutes.

In a separate saucepan, bring the stock to a boil, then reduce to a simmer.

Slowly add the hot stock to the rice, one ladle at a time, stirring continuously until it has been absorbed before adding the next ladle, until you have a creamy texture. This will take 15–20 minutes.

Spoon the Stracchino cheese and radicchio into the rice and mix through. Adjust the seasoning, if needed.

Turn off the heat, cover the pan with a lid, and leave for 3 minutes before serving. For those who really like cheese, freshly grated Parmigiano Reggiano can be added to the plates.

Note
Radicchio is renowned for being quite a bitter leaf, so for a sweeter flavor, the radicchio is soaked in water before using, as detailed above.

—Serves 4

MARIO AND ROSALIA'S WILD HOP AND FIELD HERB RISOTTO

Prep Time 10 minutes
Cooking Time 30 minutes

7 oz (200 g) wild hops (or wild or cultivated asparagus)
⅓ cup (75 ml) extra virgin olive oil
1 large onion, finely diced
4 cups (1 liter) Chicken or Vegetable Stock (pages 236–7)
1 French shallot, finely diced
1½ cups (11 oz/320 g) Vialone Nano rice (or any risotto rice)
1 cup (¾ oz/20 g) Carletti leaves (or baby spinach)
1 cup (3½ oz/100 g) grated Parmigiano Reggiano
4 tablespoons (2 oz/60 g) butter, softened
Sea salt and freshly ground black pepper

Every year our group sommelier, Cristian Casarin, and I travel to Italy to sample new wines and develop the restaurants' wine lists, and we always make an effort to stop off at his parents' house in the Veneto town of Noale. This dish has been eaten at their kitchen table on many occasions. When we're there—around Easter time—wild hops (which look like wheat) are plentiful, growing on the sides of the road and all throughout Mario and Rosalia's property. We'll meander around, picking what's needed for lunch, then catch up on the events of the year gone by. It's a joy. The core ingredients can be difficult to obtain outside Italy, but are wonderful if you can get them. Alternatively, wild or cultivated asparagus and baby spinach make great substitutes.

Chop the wild hops into 1¼ inch (3 cm) long pieces (smaller if using wild or cultivated asparagus). Heat half the olive oil in a small sauté pan over medium heat. Add the onion and wild hops and cook until the onion is golden, then remove from the pan.

Bring the stock to a boil in a large saucepan, then reduce the heat and keep at a simmer.

Heat the rest of the olive oil and the shallot in a large saucepan and cook for a few minutes until the shallot becomes translucent. Add the rice and toast over low heat for 2 minutes.

Slowly add the hot stock to the rice one ladle at a time, stirring continuously until the liquid has been absorbed before adding the next ladle. After around 8 minutes, add the sautéed hops and onion, then continue stirring and adding the stock for a further 8–10 minutes, until the rice is al dente or at your preferred level of tenderness.

Turn off the heat, add the Carletti leaves and half the Parmigiano Reggiano, and season with salt, if needed. Stir well, then add the butter on top. Cover and leave for 3 minutes. Finally, stir the butter through the risotto and serve with the remaining cheese.

—*Serves 4*

THE VENETO ✴ *Pasta, rice, and pies*

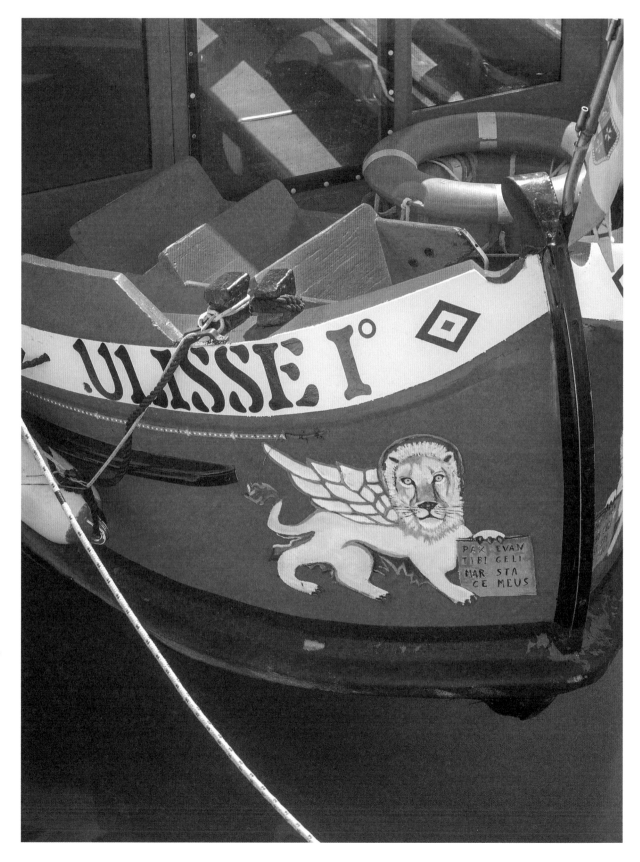

BIGOLI PASTA *with* LAKE GARDA DUCK SAUCE

Prep Time 20 minutes
Cooking Time 1 hour 45 minutes

½ cup (125 ml) extra virgin olive oil
10½ tablespoons (5½ oz/150 g) butter, diced
2 lb 4 oz (1 kg) duck legs, including thighs
1 cup (5½ oz/160 g) finely diced onion
½ cup (3 oz/80 g) finely diced carrot
½ cup (2½ oz/70 g) finely diced celery
2 garlic cloves, finely diced
1 cup (250 ml) Custoza white wine (or any fruity dry white wine)
3¼ cups (800 ml) Chicken Stock (page 236)
2 sprigs rosemary
2 sage leaves
2 bay leaves
¼ cup (60 ml) milk
14 oz (400 g) whole-wheat Bigoli dried pasta (or any large-sized whole-wheat spaghetti)
Freshly grated Parmigiano Reggiano, to serve
Sea salt and freshly ground black pepper

One of my favorite places in Italy is Lake Garda in the Veneto—particularly a little town called Costermano. The region is famous for its production of high-quality extra virgin olive oil—a long-term passion of mine. And while the towns in this area have a predominantly fish-based cuisine, much like the Venetians, they're also very big on game meat, especially duck.

Place the olive oil and half the butter in a large Dutch oven over medium heat for 2 minutes. Add the duck legs and brown evenly on all sides.

Remove the duck and add the onion, carrot, celery, and garlic. Cook until the vegetables become translucent. Season with salt and pepper.

Add the white wine and cook for a further 2 minutes, then add the chicken stock, rosemary, sage leaves, bay leaves, and milk. Return the duck to the pot. Continue cooking over low heat for 50–70 minutes or until the duck is tender. Lift out the duck and shred the meat, discarding the bones.

Cook the liquid in the pot for a further 15–25 minutes until it thickens to the consistency of a sauce, then return the shredded duck to the pot.

Bring a large pot of salted water to a rapid boil and cook the pasta for 6 minutes (until al dente) or longer, to your taste. Drain the pasta, toss with the duck ragu, and stir in the remaining diced butter.

Serve with freshly grated Parmigiano Reggiano.

Note
For an even more traditional version of this, use lard instead of butter to sauté the duck and vegetables. You can also add a small amount of cooked and chopped duck liver and giblets to the Dutch oven with the duck meat.

—Serves 4

THE VENETO ✳ *Pasta, rice, and pies*

PUMPKIN AND RICOTTA GNOCCHI *with* BLACK TRUFFLE, BROWN BUTTER, AND PARMIGIANO REGGIANO

Prep Time 25 minutes
Cooking Time 45 minutes

12½ oz (350 g) pumpkin
1 cup (9 oz/250 g) ricotta
2 eggs
¼ cup (¾ oz/25 g) finely grated pecorino cheese
2 teaspoons sea salt
¾ cup (3¾ oz/110 g) 00 flour
4 tablespoons (2 oz/60 g) butter
½ cup (⅓ oz/10 g) sage leaves
¼ cup (¾ oz/20 g) grated Parmigiano Reggiano cheese
1 piece truffle (at least ¾ oz/20 g)

This dish is an absolute joy, but it's also a labor of love. The key to getting it right is ensuring you remove as much liquid as you can from the ricotta and the pumpkin, by pat-drying with dish towels. As with any Northern Italian gnocchi, you want to avoid adding too much flour, so the more moisture you can remove, the softer and more pillowy your gnocchi will be. Have a few dish towels on hand and set some time aside. Trust me, it'll be worth the effort, and the laundry. In Italy, Berici Hills black truffles are used in this dish, but any quality black truffle will be delicious.

Preheat the oven to 350°F (180°C).

Cut the pumpkin in half, remove the seeds, place on a baking sheet, and bake for 35–40 minutes or until completely soft.

Using a spoon, scrape out the flesh to give you 9 oz (250 g) pumpkin pulp. Pat dry with dish towels as much as possible. Drain the ricotta cheese and, like the pumpkin, pat dry with dish towels as much as possible.

Place the pumpkin, ricotta, eggs, pecorino, and sea salt in a large bowl and mix together with your hands until you have a very sticky dough. Add the flour and gently fold through to make a pliable dough. If the mix is too wet, the dough will require more flour, though this can make the gnocchi tougher, so add cautiously.

Separate the dough into four equal parts and roll into thin logs. Using a knife, cut each one into 1 inch (2.5 cm) pieces. With the back of a fork or a wooden gnocchi tool, press each piece gently into the fork or tool to make an indentation.

Bring a large pot of water to a boil and add the gnocchi. When the gnocchi is cooked it will rise to the surface—lift out with a slotted spoon as it rises and drain carefully.

Meanwhile, heat the butter and sage leaves in a frying pan over medium heat. Cook until the butter is a nutty brown color and the sage is crisp.

Arrange the gnocchi on serving plates, sprinkle with the Parmigiano Reggiano, and spoon the brown butter and sage over the top. Shave black truffle over each plate and serve.

—Serves 4

RECIOTO RED WINE RISOTTO *with* LARDO

Prep Time 10 minutes
Cooking Time 35 minutes

3 cups (750 ml) Valpolicella Recioto red dessert wine (or any similar semi-sweet red dessert wine)
Scant ½ cup (100 ml) olive oil
4 French shallots, chopped
2 garlic cloves, finely sliced
1¾ cups (12½ oz/350 g) Vialone Nano rice (or any risotto rice)
3¼ cups (800 ml) Chicken Stock (page 236)
3½ oz (100 g) Grana Padano (or Parmigiano Reggiano) cheese
6 tablespoons (3 oz/80 g) butter, diced
4 oz (120 g) lardo, thinly sliced into 16 slices
Sea salt and freshly ground black pepper

This is my interpretation of the classic Veneto dish, *risotto all'Amarone.* Humbly, I prefer this one. Firstly, it requires less wine because the sweetness of the Recioto carries through the dish, and secondly, the lardo adds a beautiful saltiness and an element of indulgence. While lardo is definitely used in the Valpolicella region—where the dish originates—you'd be hard pressed to find it utilized in this way. But, blasphemous as it may be, classics can be improved! I've cooked this dish for several Venetians, and they love it.

Pour 2 cups (500 ml) of the Recioto into a small saucepan and bring to a simmer over low heat. Gently simmer until the wine has reduced by half. Allow to cool.

In a heavy-bottomed pan, heat the olive oil over low heat for 1 minute. Add the shallots and garlic and cook, stirring, for 3 minutes. Stir in the rice and continue cooking until the rice is translucent and fully coated in oil. Stir in the remaining cup of Recioto and cook for 2 minutes.

Meanwhile, in another pan, bring the chicken stock to a boil, then reduce to a simmer.

Slowly add the hot stock to the rice, one ladle at a time, stirring continuously until it has been absorbed before adding the next ladle, until you have a creamy texture. This will take 15–20 minutes.

Grate the Grana Padano into the risotto and mix through. Add the butter, stir vigorously, then season with salt and pepper. Turn the heat off, cover the pan with a lid, and leave for 3 minutes.

Spoon the risotto onto serving plates. Lay four slices of lardo over the top of each portion, then finish with a drizzle of the Recioto reduction.

—Serves 4

GAME AND MOUNTAIN HERB TORTELLINI
with MELTED HOMEMADE BUTTER AND GAME REDUCTION

Prep Time 1 hour
Cooking Time 1 hour 30 minutes

1 × 2 lb 4 oz (1 kg) pheasant (or similar game bird or rabbit), left whole
2 tablespoons extra virgin olive oil, plus extra for drizzling
1 large carrot, diced
1 large celery stalk, diced
1 large onion, diced
4 garlic cloves, minced
¼ cup (⅛ oz/5 g) rosemary leaves
6 sage leaves, 4 left whole and 2 finely chopped
6 stems wild thyme, 4 left whole and 2 picked
Generous ¾ cup (200 ml) light cream
3 cups (10½ oz/300 g) finely grated Parmigiano Reggiano
2 lb 10 oz (1.2 kg) Fresh Egg Pasta Dough, rolled into sheets no thicker than ¹⁄₁₆ inch (1 mm) (page 240)
1 egg, beaten, for egg wash
½ cup (125 ml) Cognac
Scant ¼ cup (50 ml) red wine
1 bay leaf
3 juniper berries
1⅔ cups (400 ml) Chicken Stock (page 236)
4 tablespoons (2 oz/60 g) Home-Made Butter (page 243)
Sea salt and freshly ground black pepper

This is a classic Northern Italian dish that you will find outside the Veneto area, stretching from Piedmonte all the way across to Friuli, and it's one of my all-time favorite things to eat. Here we use pheasant, but any game product, including rabbit, venison, quail, and wild boar, can be a substitute.

Preheat the oven to 350°F (180°C).

Season the pheasant thoroughly with salt and pepper. Heat the olive oil in a large frying pan for 2 minutes, then add the pheasant and brown all over.

In a roasting pan, combine the carrot, celery, onion, three-quarters of the garlic, the rosemary, 4 whole sage leaves, and 4 wild thyme sprigs. Drizzle with a little olive oil. Place the pheasant on top and roast in the oven for 45 minutes.

Strip the meat off the bird. Using a butcher's cleaver or large knife, cut the carcass into small pieces and set aside. Finely dice the meat, allow to cool, then refrigerate.

Mix the diced pheasant meat with the chopped sage and thyme leaves, cream, and Parmigiano Reggiano. Add salt and pepper if needed.

To make the tortellini, cut the pasta into 2 inch (5 cm) circles and add a teaspoon of pheasant mix to the middle of each. Using a pastry brush, wet one side of each pasta circle with egg wash, then fold over to form a half-moon shape. Finally, bring the two ends to meet to form tortellini.

To make the game reduction, remove the whole sage leaves and thyme stems from the roasting pan and reserve. Add the chopped pheasant carcass to the pan and return to the oven. Cook for 20 minutes or until brown. Add the Cognac and a little of the red wine to deglaze the pan.

Spoon all the ingredients from the roasting pan into a saucepan and add the reserved whole sage leaves and thyme stems. Add the rest of the red wine, the remaining garlic, and the bay leaf and juniper berries. Cook over low heat until reduced to a syrup consistency, then add the chicken stock and cook until reduced to a third of its volume. Pass through a fine sieve and season with salt and pepper if needed.

Bring a large pot of water to a boil and add 2 tablespoons salt. Cook the tortellini in the boiling water until they float. In a large frying pan, melt the butter and toss the drained tortellini in the butter.

Serve the tortellini drizzled with the melted butter and the game reduction.

—*Serves 4*

Mains

DRUNKEN CHICKEN AND MOUNTAIN MUSHROOM FRICASSEE *with* RED CORN POLENTA

Prep Time 20 minutes, plus 24 hours marinating
Cooking Time 1 hour 20 minutes

4½ lb (2 kg) whole chickens, spatchcocked
10 pearl onions, peeled
1 carrot, finely diced
1 celery stalk, finely diced
4 garlic cloves, finely diced
1 bottle Padovan Novello red wine (or any light-bodied red wine)
½ cup (125 ml) Cognac
Generous ½ cup (150 ml) extra virgin olive oil
4 cups (1 liter) Chicken Stock (page 236)
3½ oz (100 g) fresh chanterelle mushrooms, sliced (or shimeji or portobello mushrooms)
2 sprigs rosemary
1 cup (6½ oz/190 g) coarse red corn (Storo) or yellow polenta cornmeal
2 oz (60 g) Parmigiano Reggiano
7 tablespoons (3½ oz/100 g) butter
Fresh herbs, to garnish
Sea salt and freshly ground black pepper

This is a Padovan version of the iconic French dish, *coq au vin*—a beautiful wintery, indulgent dish for the family. It's essential that the chicken is marinated for 24 hours, allowing the flavors of the red wine and Cognac to seep into the meat, imparting a stunning and intense flavor.

Cut the spatchcocked chickens into quarters (legs and breasts), with the breasts left on the bone. In a large bowl, combine the chicken, vegetables, garlic, red wine, and Cognac. Cover and refrigerate for 24 hours.

Remove the bowl from the refrigerator and strain, reserving the marinade. Pat the chicken and vegetables dry with paper towels, reserving the wine and Cognac.

Heat the oil in a large Dutch oven for 2 minutes over medium heat. Add the chicken pieces, skin-side-down, and brown the skin. Turn and sear for 2 more minutes. Remove the chicken and set aside.

Add the strained onions, carrot, celery, and garlic to the pot and cook for 4 minutes over medium heat, stirring continuously. Add the red wine and Cognac and cook for 30 minutes, until reduced by half.

Preheat the oven to 350°F (180°C).

Return the chicken to the pot and season with salt and pepper. Add the chicken stock, mushrooms, and rosemary and bring to a boil.

Transfer the pot to the oven and cook for 35–40 minutes. Taste and adjust the seasoning, adding more salt and pepper if needed.

Meanwhile, bring 4 cups (1 liter) water to a boil in a large pot and slowly add the polenta in a steady stream, stirring continuously. Cook, stirring, for 40 minutes. Add the cheese and butter and season with salt. Mix thoroughly, then cover with a lid and leave for 5 minutes.

Spoon the soft polenta onto a serving plate and add the chicken, vegetables, and sauce. Garnish with any fresh herbs.

—Serves 4

ROASTED BASSANO TROUT, HOMEMADE BUTTER, AND SAGE *with* BORLOTTI BEAN AND POTATO PURÉE

Prep Time 20 minutes, plus overnight soaking of the borlotti beans
Cooking Time 1 hour 10 minutes

1 cup (7 oz/200 g) dried borlotti beans
1½ cups (375 ml) Bassano extra virgin olive oil (or any quality extra virgin olive oil), plus extra for the fish
1 French shallot, finely diced
2 garlic cloves, finely diced
1 cup (¾ oz/20 g) sage leaves
1 lb 5 oz (600 g) quality mashing potatoes
Generous ½ cup (150 ml) Buttermilk (page 243)
Scant ½ cup (100 ml) light cream
4 × 1 lb 3 oz–1 lb 9 oz (550 g–700 g) trout, cleaned and scaled
7 tablespoons (3½ oz/100 g) Homemade Butter (page 243)
Juice of 1 lemon
Sage flowers or any edible flowers or herbs, to garnish
Sea salt and freshly ground black pepper

This dish hails from Bassano, and celebrates the region's remarkable local river trout, made all the more enjoyable with homemade butter. It's worth the effort to make your own, and it's not nearly as daunting as some think. Don't let the process distract you from the cooking of the fish though. One of my all-time favorite things to eat is whole fish, cooked on the bone. Take care, however, since it quickly loses its appeal when overcooked.

Place the dried borlotti beans in a pot and add 10 cups (2.5 liters) of water. Bring to a boil and cook for 3 minutes. Remove from the heat, allow to cool, drain, and then cover with fresh water. Leave in the refrigerator overnight.

Drain and rinse the beans.

Pour ½ cup (125 ml) of the oil into a saucepan and heat on the stovetop. Add the French shallot, garlic, and a third of the sage and gently sauté until the shallot and garlic are translucent. Do not add salt.

Add the borlotti beans and just cover with cold water.

Bring to a boil, then turn the heat down to a simmer. Cover the pan and cook for 45 minutes until the beans are tender. Transfer to a blender or food processor and blend to a purée.

Meanwhile, wash, peel, and quarter the potatoes. You want the beans and potatoes to finish cooking at the same time, so the potatoes need to start cooking about 20 minutes after the beans. Put them in a large pot and cover with cold water. Add ½ tablespoon salt and cook over medium heat for 20–25 minutes or until soft. Drain the potatoes.

In another small pan, heat the buttermilk, cream, and generous ¾ cup (200 ml) of the olive oil. Bring up to high heat but do not allow to boil. Add the buttermilk mixture to the hot drained potatoes and mix with a wooden spoon. Push the potato mixture through a ricer and then a sieve into a large bowl. Add the borlotti bean purée and mix together.

Preheat the oven to 400°F (200°C).

To make the roasted Bassano river trout, score across the body of the whole fish with a sharp knife, making about five incisions ½ inch (1 cm) deep on each side of the fish.

Rub the trout outside and inside the scoring cuts and inside the cavity with 5 tablespoons (2½ oz/70 g) of the butter, ensuring the fish have a generous covering. Season with sea salt and ground black pepper to taste. Place a sage leaf in each of the score incisions and then place two additional sage leaves in the cavity of each fish.

Put the remaining butter and oil on a baking sheet and heat in the oven until the butter starts to bubble.

Arrange the trout on the hot tray and roast in the oven for 6 minutes. Turn the fish over and roast for another 4–5 minutes, taking care not to overcook the fish. Remember that the fish will continue to cook after it is taken out of the oven—the goal is to have the fish just cooked and with a crispy, buttery skin.

Remove the trout and deglaze the tray with the lemon juice. Serve the trout on a bed of the potato and borlotti bean purée and pour the pan juices over the top of the fish. Garnish with sage flowers, or any edible flowers or herbs.

—Serves 4

SPIT-ROASTED VICENZA GUINEA FOWL
with POMEGRANATE AND WILD HERB MISTICANZA SALAD

Prep Time 20 minutes
Cooking Time 1 hour

2 pomegranates
1 × 2 lb 4 oz (1 kg) guinea fowl (or chicken, game bird, duck, or pheasant)
¼ cup (⅛ oz/5 g) sage leaves
7 tablespoons (3½ oz/100 g) Homemade Butter, softened (page 243)
1 lemon
1 whole head of garlic
Scant ½ cup (100 ml) extra virgin olive oil
Sea salt and freshly ground black pepper

Misticanza salad
8 cups (2 lb/900 g) mixed salad greens, herbs, and edible flowers
Juice of 1 lemon
Juice of 1 orange
Scant ½ cup (100 ml) Agrumato lemon extra virgin olive oil

In Vicenza this recipe is often made with baby turkey in place of guinea fowl, and it's a common sight on dining tables at family feasts throughout the Christmas season. The spit-roasting process—the best for roasting meats—provides short bursts of intense heat. Because the meat is being cooked on the bone, you end up with the most succulent, flavorful result.

For the guinea fowl, preheat a spit roast to high, or the oven to 400°F (200°C).

To prepare the pomegranates, cut in half and hold one-half over a bowl, cut-side-down. Using a wooden spoon, tap the skin side of the fruit and the seeds will fall out into the bowl. Remove any white pith from the seeds.

Reserve half of the pomegranate seeds for the salad. Crush the remaining seeds with a potato masher and then strain through a fine strainer to obtain the juice.

To prepare the guinea fowl, use your fingers to carefully separate the skin from the flesh on the breasts to make a pocket. Place half the sage leaves and the softened butter under the skin and season with salt and pepper.

Cut the lemon and the head of garlic in half and place in the body cavity of the bird with the remaining sage. Season with salt and pepper. Rub the outside of the bird with the olive oil and season with salt and pepper.

Place the bird onto the spit and secure according to the manufacturer's instructions. Place the spit as close to the flame as possible and cook for 40–60 minutes, basting the bird with pomegranate juice every 10 minutes or so.

Alternatively, roast the bird in the oven in a roasting pan for 15 minutes, then lower the heat to 350°F (180°C) and roast for a further 35–45 minutes, basting every 10 minutes, until the juices run clear when you pierce the thigh with a knife.

When the bird is cooked, remove from the spit or oven, cover with foil, and leave in a warm place for 20 minutes.

To make the misticanza salad, wash and dry the salad greens. Pick the herb leaves off the stems and toss with the salad leaves and edible flowers.

Mix the lemon juice, orange juice, and lemon olive oil and season with sea salt and pepper. Toss the salad leaves, herbs, edible flowers, and pomegranate seeds with the lemon and orange dressing.

Carve the guinea fowl into four portions, drizzle with the remaining pomegranate juice, and serve with the misticanza salad.

Note
Guinea fowl is a specialty game bird that can be difficult to source. Specialty butchers might be able to order them, even if they don't regularly stock them.

—Serves 4

VERONESE BEEF AND CHERRY PASTISSADA
with CELERIAC AND PANCETTA GRATIN

Prep Time 30 minutes
Cooking Time 3 hours

Beef and cherry pastissada
4 tablespoons extra virgin olive oil
2 lb 4 oz (1 kg) boneless beef
    shank
1½ cups (350 ml) Valpolicella
    DOC red wine (or any
    medium-bodied red wine)
4 cups (1 liter) Beef Stock
    (page 237)
2 garlic cloves, minced
1 bay leaf
1 cinnamon stick
2 teaspoons mustard powder
Juice of 1 orange
Juice of 1 lemon
1 teaspoon raw sugar
1 teaspoon freshly ground
    black pepper
1 lb 5 oz (600 g) ripe fresh
    (Veronese) cherries, pitted
1 tablespoon (½ oz/15 g) butter
Sea salt and freshly ground
    black pepper

Celeriac and pancetta gratin
2 lb 4 oz (1 kg) celeriac
    (celery root), peeled and cut
    into ¼ inch (5 mm) thick slices
4 tablespoons (2 oz/60 g) butter,
    plus extra for brushing
3½ oz (100 g) rolled pancetta,
    thinly sliced and diced into
    ¼ inch (5 mm) pieces
1 onion, finely diced
1 garlic clove, finely diced
3½ oz (100 g) Parmigiano
    Reggiano, grated

The traditional version of this dish, by which my recipe is inspired, is *pastissada de caval*. It was, and still is, made traditionally with horse meat. This is the most important dish of Verona, a region where equine butchers are more prevalent than conventional butchers. This recipe is a more modern version, using beef as the meat and fresh cherries from the Veronese hills. It's served with a wonderful gratin of pancetta and celeriac—the latter being almost exclusively cultivated in the province of Verona, to the point where it is often referred to as "the celery of Verona."

Preheat the oven to 325°F (170°C).

To make the *pastissada*, heat a deep Dutch oven over high heat. Add the oil and heat for 2 minutes, then add the beef shank and brown on all sides.

Add the red wine and cook until almost evaporated. Add the beef stock, garlic, bay leaf, cinnamon, mustard powder, orange and lemon juice, sugar, and pepper and stir thoroughly. Cover the pot and transfer to the oven. Cook for 2 hours, turning the meat frequently.

Add the cherries to the pot, cover, and cook for a further 30 minutes.

Meanwhile, to make the gratin, bring a pot of water to a boil, add the celeriac, and blanch for 2 minutes, then drain.

Heat the butter in a sauté pan over low heat and cook the pancetta, onion, and garlic until the onion has softened and is fully cooked.

Divide the Parmigiano Reggiano in half, keeping half to top the dish.

Arrange a layer of celeriac neatly over the base of a baking dish, brush with butter, and season with salt and pepper. Scatter with a little pancetta, onion, and garlic mix, and grated Parmigiano. Repeat the layers until you have used up all the ingredients, finishing with the reserved Parmigiano.

Remove the beef from the oven, turn the temperature up to 400°F (200°C), and bake the gratin for 20 minutes until golden brown.

Strain the liquid from the Dutch oven into a pan and simmer over low heat on the stovetop until it has reduced and thickened to the consistency of a sauce. Reheat the beef and cherries in the sauce and then lift out onto plates. Whisk the butter into the sauce just before serving, and spoon over the meat and cherries. Serve with the gratin.

—*Serves 4*

"LESSO" VERONESE COTECHINO SAUSAGE AND MIXED CUTS *with* PEARA AND CREN SALSAS

Prep Time 30 minutes (the salsa cren to be prepared 2 weeks in advance)
Cooking Time 3 hours 30 minutes

1 onion, chopped into large pieces
2 carrots, chopped into
    large pieces
4 celery stalks, chopped into
    large pieces
2 bay leaves
10 peppercorns
1 veal shank
10½ oz (300 g) pork belly,
    bone-in
14 oz (400 g) cotechino sausage
½ stewing chicken

Salsa cren
14 oz (400 g) horseradish root
Scant ¼ cup (1½ oz/40 g) sugar
2 teaspoons salt
2 cups (500 ml) white
    wine vinegar

Salsa peara
3½ oz (100 g) bone marrow
4 tablespoons (2 oz/60 g) butter
1–2 cups (250–500 ml) Beef
    or Veal Stock (page 237)
1 cup (2 oz/60 g) dried
    breadcrumbs
Whole peppercorns, to taste
2 oz (60 g) Parmigiano Reggiano,
    grated (optional)
Sea salt and freshly ground
    black pepper

Known as *lesso* or *bollito misto*, this is another example of classic Northern Italian winter fare and is a personal favorite of mine. The Veronese version utilizes particular condiments, including *cren* (freshly grated horseradish in salt and a little sugar) and *peara* (a bone marrow and bread sauce with black pepper). The quantity of black pepper is a subject of great conjecture and is completely at the discretion of the cook. With pepper being one of my favorite ingredients, I say be generous!

To make the *salsa cren*, grate the horseradish into a mixing bowl, then stir in the sugar and salt. Place in an airtight sterilized jar, then pour the white wine vinegar over to cover. Seal the jar and leave for 2 weeks to marinate.

Place the onion, carrot, celery, bay leaves, peppercorns, veal shank, pork belly, and cotechino sausage into a large stockpot and cover with 16 cups (4 liters) water. Bring to a boil, then lower the heat to a simmer and cook for 1 hour, skimming off the excess fat from the top throughout the cooking time. The cotechino will be quite salty, so check the cooking liquid after 30 minutes to see if it requires further seasoning (it shouldn't).

After 1 hour, lift out the cotechino and place in a bowl with enough poaching liquid to cover it. Cook the meats and vegetables in the stockpot for a further 1 hour.

Add the chicken to the stockpot and add more water if needed to cover the meats. Check the seasoning again and simmer again for 1 hour.

Return the cotechino to the stockpot, bring to a boil, then reduce the heat and simmer for a further 20 minutes.

To make the *salsa peara*, place a small pan over low heat. Add the bone marrow and butter and allow to melt. Pour in the stock, stirring continuously, then mix in the breadcrumbs. Cook slowly for at least 1½ hours. Season with ground pepper, whole peppercorns, and sea salt: the amount of pepper used is personal preference. Freshly grated Parmigiano is also a great addition to *salsa peara*.

Slice the meat and serve with the vegetables and two salsas as condiments.

Notes
This recipe is really another version of nutrient-rich bone broth, often used to cook vegetables and legumes such as lentils. To increase the nutritional value of this dish, the braising liquid can be replaced with unseasoned beef bone stock.

The *cren* recipe will make a lot more than is needed here. Store the remainder in an airtight container in the fridge: it will keep for a long time and can be used whenever horseradish is called for. It's beautiful served with steak or oily fish, such as salmon and trout.

—*Serves 4*

THE VENETO ✳ *Mains*

VEAL CHEEKS *with* MILK RISOTTO CAKES, SAVOY CABBAGE, AND CHESTNUTS

Prep Time 20 minutes, plus 1 hour for chilling the risotto cakes
Cooking Time 4 hours 30 minutes

4 × 9 oz (250 g) veal cheeks (or beef cheeks), cleaned of excess fat
Generous ½ cup (150 ml) extra virgin olive oil
1 carrot, diced
1 celery stalk, diced
2 onions, diced
4 garlic cloves, sliced
1 tablespoon tomato paste
1¼ cups (300 ml) Euganean Chardonnay DOP (or any good chardonnay)
Scant 3 cups (700 ml) Beef, Veal, or Chicken Stock (pages 236–7)
2 sprigs rosemary
2 bay leaves
Sea salt and freshly ground black pepper

Milk risotto cakes
5 cups (1.2 liters) milk
¾ cup (5½ oz/150 g) Vialone Nano rice (or any risotto rice)
2 oz (60 g) Parmigiano Reggiano, grated
5 tablespoons (2½ oz/70 g) butter
1 egg, lightly beaten
Extra virgin olive oil, for cooking

Savoy cabbage and chestnuts
9 oz (250 g) raw whole chestnuts
¼ savoy cabbage
8½ tablespoons (4¼ oz/120 g) butter
5½ oz (150 g) rolled pancetta, diced
Olive oil, for cooking

In the Veneto, *risotto latte* was always considered *cucina povera*, or "food of the poor." The milk risotto was a breakfast staple for many working-class Italians and its simplicity made it the perfect comfort food. Like a lot of "poor people's" food, it tastes fantastic. I've given it a modern makeover here, converting it into risotto cakes and serving them with an absolutely stunning product (if you can get your hands on it): veal cheeks. If you don't have any luck at the butcher, beef cheeks make a great substitute.

Preheat the oven to 315°F (160°C).

Season the veal with salt and pepper.

Heat half the olive oil in a Dutch oven over medium heat for 3 minutes, then add the veal cheeks and brown all over for 3–4 minutes. Remove and set aside.

Add the carrot, celery, and onion to the pot and cook for 5 minutes or until the vegetables become translucent. Add the garlic and tomato paste and cook again for 2 minutes.

Return the veal cheeks to the pot and pour over the wine and stock. Add the rosemary and bay leaves and cover. Place in the oven and cook for 3½–4 hours until the veal is very tender and comes apart with the pressure of a fork.

Meanwhile, prepare the milk risotto cakes and cabbage.

To make the milk risotto cakes, pour the milk into a saucepan and season with salt and pepper. Bring to a simmer over medium heat, stirring continuously with a flat-bottomed wooden spoon.

Add the rice and cook for 15 minutes. The milk should slowly bubble through the cooking process and the rice and milk should slowly thicken. Stir continuously to avoid the milk and rice sticking to the bottom of the pan and burning.

When the rice is cooked, add the Parmigiano and 1½ tablespoons (¾ oz/20 g) of the butter and stir to thoroughly combine. Cover the pan and set aside to cool, then refrigerate for at least 1 hour.

Mix the egg into the cold milk risotto. Use your hands to roll into balls of about 3 oz (80 g) each: the recipe should make about 8 balls. Press the balls gently to flatten them to about half their height. Place on a baking sheet and cover with a dish towel.

To prepare the savoy cabbage, place the chestnuts in a saucepan and cover with water. Bring to a gentle boil and cook for 20 minutes or until they are soft in the center. Set the chestnuts aside to cool. When cool enough to handle, peel off the outer shells.

Cut the cabbage into quarters, remove the core, and cut into ¾ inch (2 cm) strips.

Melt 5 tablespoons (2½ oz/70 g) of the butter in a saucepan over medium heat. Add the pancetta and cook until crisp, then season with salt and pepper. Add the cabbage and allow to fully wilt, then cook for a further 2–3 minutes.

To cook the risotto cakes, place a small non-stick pan over medium–high heat and add 3½ tablespoons (1¾ oz/50 g) butter and a little olive oil. When the butter begins to foam, add the risotto cakes and fry for 2–3 minutes or until golden brown and crisp. Flip and repeat on the other side, ensuring the cakes are hot in the center.

In another pan, add the remaining 3½ tablespoons (1¾ oz/50 g) butter and a little olive oil and cook the chestnuts until they caramelize and are golden in color, then season with salt and pepper.

Once the veal is cooked, remove from the Dutch oven and cover. Strain the cooking liquid into another saucepan and simmer over low heat until reduced to the consistency of a light sauce.

Return the veal cheeks to the sauce to heat through before serving. Serve with the risotto cakes, cabbage and caramelized chestnuts, and veal sauce.

—Serves 4

Dolci

VENETIAN CARNIVAL FRITTERS

Prep Time 10 minutes, plus 1 hour soaking raisins
Cooking Time 10 minutes

1½ cups (9 oz/250 g) raisins
4 cups (1 lb 2 oz/500 g) 00 flour,
    plus extra for dusting
4 eggs, separated into yolks and
    whites
2 teaspoons baking powder
2 cups (14 oz/400 g) sugar
Scant ½ cup (100 ml) rum
Juice and zest of 1 orange
Zest of 1 lemon
¾ cup (175 ml) vegetable oil
¾ cup (175 ml) milk
8½ cups (2 liters) grapeseed
    oil, for frying

You will find these in the *pasticcerie* throughout the whole of the Veneto during the annual *Carnevale* period—a time of particular indulgence and excess every January. This version is fantastic, but an equally beautiful iteration is made without raisins and with a custard center. These are best served warm with an espresso (and good luck stopping at one).

Soak the raisins in warm water for 1 hour, drain, and dry on paper towels, then dust with a little flour to absorb any excess moisture.

In a large mixing bowl, mix together the flour, egg yolks, baking powder, and half the sugar. Add the rum, orange juice and zest, lemon zest, vegetable oil, milk, and raisins and beat until smooth.

Measure out the egg whites— you need ¼ cup (60 ml). Beat until stiff, then fold through the batter.

Heat the grapeseed oil in deep pan or deep fryer to 350°F (180°C).

Using a tablespoon, drop spoonfuls of the batter into the hot oil and cook for 2–3 minutes until brown. Turn and cook for 2–3 minutes on the other side.

Remove the fritters from the oil and roll in the remaining sugar to serve.

—Serves 8

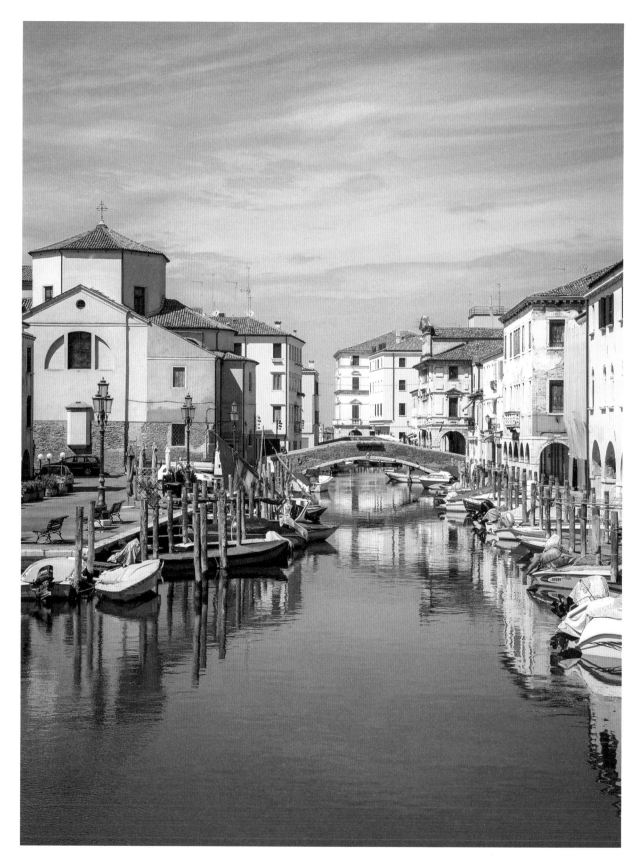

PANDORO TIRAMISU *with* HOMEMADE MASCARPONE

Prep Time 10 minutes, plus overnight refrigeration, if desired

4 egg yolks
2 tablespoons sugar
2 egg whites
2 cups (1 lb/450 g) Mascarpone
    (page 243)
2 cups (500 ml) strong
    black coffee
Scant ½ cup (100 ml) Marsala
    wine
½ *pandoro*
3 tablespoons dark cocoa powder

Pandoro is Veronese Italian Christmas cake and is a variation of the famous *panettone*, which literally translates to "big bread," thanks to its filling of raisins and citrus zest. *Pandoro*, or "bread of gold," differs as it has no zest or raisins. Here I use it in an unusual way as part of another classic Italian dessert that hails from the Veneto's Treviso region: tiramisu.

Whisk the egg yolks and sugar in a large mixing bowl until pale and creamy.

Whisk the egg whites in a separate bowl until stiff.

Mix the mascarpone into the egg yolk mixture. Fold in half of the egg whites and then fold in the remaining egg whites.

Combine the coffee and Marsala.

Slice the *pandoro* into ¾ inch (2 cm) thick slices.

You will need a glass bowl 9 inches (23 cm) in diameter and 4 inches (10 cm) deep. Lay half the *pandoro* slices over the base of the bowl. Drizzle half the coffee over the *pandoro*. Pour half the mascarpone mixture over the top.

Repeat the layers, using up all the ingredients, then dust with cocoa.

This can be served immediately but, for best results, refrigerate overnight first.

—Serves 4

VALPOLICELLA SPICED PEARS *with* SWEET CREAM

Prep Time 30 minutes
Cooking Time 1 hour

4 pears
1 bottle Valpolicella DOC red wine (or any good-quality medium-bodied red wine)
⅓ cup (2½ oz/75 g) brown sugar
1 cinnamon stick
4 black peppercorns
2 cloves
Juice of 1 orange
Zest of ½ orange
1 sprig rosemary
1 vanilla bean
4 tablespoons pistachios, roasted and chopped

Sweet cream
½ cup (4 oz/115 g) Mascarpone (page 243)
½ cup (125 ml) heavy whipping cream
Zest of ½ lemon
2 tablespoons confectioners' sugar

This is a simple, yet stunning, dessert. It showcases one of Italy's most revered wine appellations, Valpolicella, where vine cultivation is said to be traced back to the fifth century BC. Produced in the Veneto, Valpolicella is one of the most beloved red wines in Italy, recognized for its rich black cherry and cranberry aromas and soft tannins. And while it makes for exceptional drinking, it's very commonly cooked with in and around Venice, including in the national dish of slow-cooked beef stew, *pastissada*, as well as in a number of desserts.

Peel the pears and slice in half lengthwise, then remove the cores with a melon baller or small teaspoon, keeping the stalks intact for presentation.

In a saucepan, combine the red wine, brown sugar, cinnamon, peppercorns, cloves, orange juice, orange zest, and rosemary.

Cut the vanilla bean in half lengthwise and scrape out the seeds. Place the vanilla pod and half the seeds in the pan with the wine mixture (reserving the remaining seeds for the sweet cream).

Place the saucepan over medium heat and bring to a simmer, then add the pears and cook for 1 hour until tender. Remove the pan from the heat and let the pears cool in the poaching liquid.

For the sweet cream, combine the mascarpone, cream, lemon zest, sugar, and remaining vanilla seeds in a mixing bowl and whisk until the mixture is like lightly whipped cream.

Serve the pears either warm or chilled, with the sweet cream and garnished with the pistachios and a little of the poaching liquid.

—Serves 4

WILD BERRIES IN RECIOTO BIANCO *with* GRAPPA MASCARPONE *and* SAVOIARDI COOKIES

Prep Time 20 minutes (the cookies are best baked 24 hours in advance)
Cooking Time 15 minutes

Savoiardi cookies (lady fingers)
4 egg whites
Generous ½ cup (4 oz/120 g) sugar, plus 2 tablespoons for sprinkling
6 egg yolks
Scant 1 cup (4 oz/120 g) all-purpose flour, sifted
2 tablespoons confectioners' sugar

Poli Museo grappa mascarpone
1 vanilla bean
Generous ¾ cup (185 ml) heavy whipping cream
2 tablespoons sugar
1 tablespoon Poli Museo grappa (or any quality grappa)
¾ cup (6½ oz/185 g) Mascarpone (page 243)

Wild berries in Recioto Bianco
½ tablespoon Ligurian bee honey (or any quality honey)
½ cup (125 ml) Recioto Bianco wine (or any semi-sweet white dessert wine)
3 cups (14½ oz/415 g) mixed wild berries

Simplicity at its best, this dessert is also a great celebration of the Veneto region's wine and spirit industries. The Recioto Bianco is a sweet wine made from Garganega grapes, usually from an area called Soave, renowned for its eponymous wine. Another beautiful inclusion is the Poli Museo grappa, aged in barrels for 25 years: an absolutely stunning product that is a perfect companion to fresh mascarpone.

To make the savoiardi cookies, preheat the oven to 375°F (190°C).

Whisk the egg whites with half the sugar until stiff peaks form.

In another bowl, beat the egg yolks with the remaining sugar for 5 minutes until a pale cream color.

Fold half the egg white mixture into the egg yolk mixture. Fold in the flour. Fold the remaining egg white into the egg yolk mixture.

Line a baking sheet with parchment paper and dust with confectioners' sugar. Place the batter into a pastry bag and pipe finger shapes, about 3 inches (7.5 cm) long, onto the sheet, spacing the lady fingers 1 inch (2.5 cm) apart.

Sprinkle the cookies with 2 tablespoons sugar and bake for 7 minutes.

To make the Poli Museo grappa mascarpone, cut the vanilla bean in half lengthwise and scrape out the seeds. Place half the seeds in a mixing bowl (keeping the pod and remaining seeds for the wild berries in Recioto Bianco). Add the cream and sugar to the bowl and whisk until lightly whipped.

Mix together the grappa and mascarpone, add to the bowl, and fold in.

To make the wild berries in Recioto Bianco, combine the honey with the reserved vanilla seeds and pod in a small saucepan. Gently stir over low heat until the honey becomes a thin liquid. Pour in the wine and gently stir with a wooden spoon until completely mixed. Set aside and allow to cool.

continued...

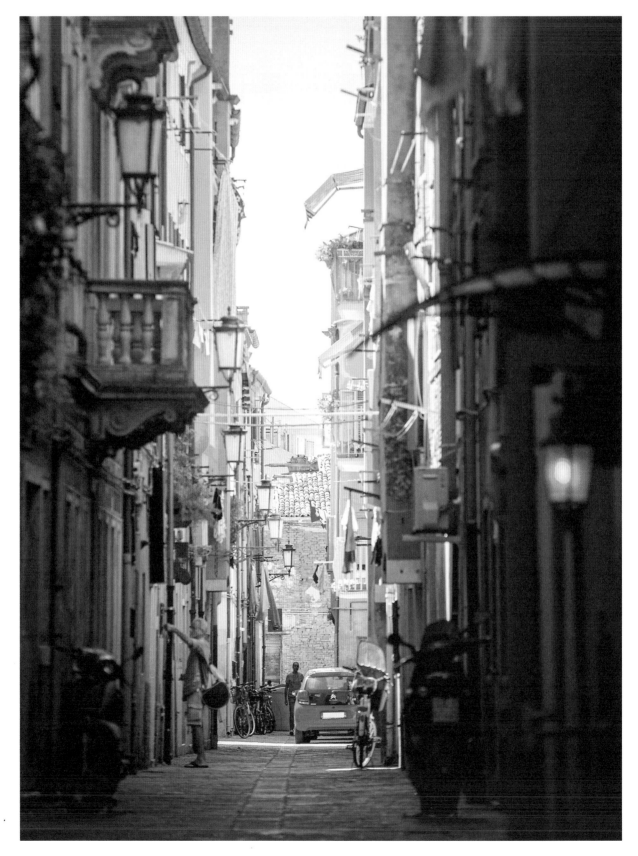

Wash and prepare the berries by removing the stalks and cutting any large berries in half. Gently pat the berries dry and place in a mixing bowl.

Spoon 4 tablespoons of the Recioto Bianco and honey sauce into the bowl with the berries, mixing carefully so that the sauce covers all the berries. A little more sauce can be poured over the berries when serving.

Serve in glass coupes. Spoon a little of the Poli Museo mascarpone cream into the bottom of the coupes, divide the berries evenly between the coupes, and add a little more of the mascarpone cream on top. Serve with savoiardi cookies to finish.

Notes
For best results, bake the savoiardi cookies a day in advance and keep in an airtight container.

The Recioto and honey recipe will make more than this recipe requires, but this sauce will keep for a long time in an airtight container in the fridge.

—Serves 4

VENETIAN CROATIA

III

A MARITIME SUPERHIGHWAY

Simply put, without secure passage and control through the waters in and around the Croatian coast, Venice wouldn't have become what she did.

Spanning a great length of the Adriatic Sea, the Croatian coastline was a significant component of the footprint the Venetians needed to cross in order to trade with the East. Sitting between Venice and her key historical trading territories—particularly Greece and the Levant—it linked the Republic with some of her greatest wealth-generating products: cotton, wheat, spices, silk, and the ash used for glass making (today an unrivaled industry in Venice). So, this region was critical.

The Croatian coastline and islands were the first lands claimed as part of the Republic's international expansion, and they were an absolutely essential win. Not only did this allow the Venetians to maintain their trading monopoly by removing competitive industries on the Croatian coast, the area also provided Venetians with the manpower, money, and resources necessary for the next leg of their journey. And the Venetians were more than comfortable here. Like Venice, the Croatian coast is an archipelago, so Venice's boats would weave and wind through these stunningly beautiful island waterways, taking advantage of the ports along the way to pick up resources to either trade or take back home.

Venice ruled the Croatian coast for about 700 years, ending in the late 18th century. Although the Croatians are clearly and proudly their own people, distinctively independent with their own long and unique history, Venice's legacy can still very much be seen. Walk around the islands and the coast today and the winged lion—the symbol of the Venetian Republic—is scattered throughout, perched on top of the city gate of Zadar, the City Lodge of Loggia on Hvar, and on the clock tower in Rovinj, known to this day as Croatia's "Little Venice."

Croatia had an impact on Venice too and the intercultural exchange traversed all sorts of things, not least of which was the bounty from its land and sea. Learned Venetians today will tell you that the famous Venetian dish of *scampi alla busara* is actually Istrian in origin. As is Istrian stone, or *pietra d'Istria*, the most prevalent stone in Venetian architecture, some of which proudly adorns the iconic ruler's (Doge's) palace in the Piazza San Marco.

Out of everything, however, food is where the Venetian influence is most visible. For me, eating on these islands and along the coast feels like eating in Italy. And how stunningly masterful they are at cooking this way, for if the Venetians brought influential recipes and culinary ideas, the Croatians have clearly shown that they understand them and have made them their own. Like with quality regional Italian cooking, it's usually pretty simple, but in the main, it's some of the best food in the world.

As you move inland, the influence becomes noticeably more Slavic. The food of the coast and islands, however, is indisputably Venetian influenced. They eat pasta and risotto like Venetians and Northern Italians do. Fish and seafood dominate and are often treated almost identically to how they are in Venice. Squid ink risotto, sweet pea risotto, the seafood stew known as *brodet* (*brodetto* in Italian), traditionally served over polenta, and beautifully simple pasta with truffles are national dishes seen absolutely everywhere along the Croatian coast. Close your eyes and taste the food: it's different, but you really could be in Italy. And it's not just what they eat; it's how they eat too. A meal on the Croatian coast typically comprises an antipasto (often locally made gently smoked charcuterie), then a pasta or risotto, followed by a main course, and, to conclude, something sweet. Sound familiar? Without question, this is an Italian scheme of eating.

Travel south to Greece and its islands and it all changes quite dramatically. As you'll see in this book's final chapter, whilst much of Greece is heavily influenced by the Venetians, Greeks don't really eat like the Italians. Croatians do.

While seafood dominates the cuisine of the Croatian coast, it is a curious fact that it's a meat dish that coastal Croatia is most proud of: *pašticada*. Venetian influence? Of course. *Pašticada* is believed to have first originated in the Veneto— Verona, in fact—where in AD 489 the Goth king, Theodoric, won sovereignty for the city by overcoming barbarian enemies in an epic battle that saw a significant horse mortality rate. After the battle, the horse carcasses were given to the community and butchered, then the meat mixed with wine and aromatics before slow cooking. *Pašticada de caval* was born.

While horsemeat is still widely consumed in the Veneto today, most commonly in *pastissada de caval*, the use of beef in the dish *pastissada de manzo* is far more common in Venice, and is very similar to the *pašticada* of Croatia. Continue down the Adriatic and you'll find similar *pastissada*-inspired dishes; for example *pastitsada* in Corfu, the Greek island that also played a key role in the administration and defense of the Venetian Republic's critical trade routes. While each of these iterations has its own nuances, most share at least a few of the following key aromatics: pepper, cinnamon, cloves, bay leaves, and nutmeg, which, as you now know, were riches acquired by the Venetians from the East.

Some of my absolute favorite recipes from this book reside in this chapter. Some of my favorite recipes of all time, in fact. Stunning food from a stunning place.

VENETIAN CROATIA

DALMATIAN WOOD-GRILLED CALAMARI
with RED PEPPER MAYONNAISE, PARSLEY, AND ONION SALAD

Prep Time 20 minutes, plus 4 hours for marinating the calamari
Cooking Time 20 minutes

Wood-grilled calamari
1 lb 2 oz (500 g) calamari
½ cup (125 ml) quality early-
   harvest extra virgin olive oil
2 garlic cloves, sliced

Red pepper mayonnaise
4 red peppers
Scant ¼ cup (2 oz/60 g)
   Mayonnaise (page 241)
Sea salt and freshly ground
   black pepper

Parsley and onion salad
2 cups (1½ oz/40 g) Italian parsley
   leaves
½ cup (2 oz/60 g) finely sliced
   red onion
¼ cup (60 ml) extra virgin
   olive oil
¼ cup (60 ml) lemon juice

This dish is a wonderful example of classic Dalmatian cooking, in which calamari is almost always grilled over coals or wood. Having said that, a barbecue or chargrill will deliver a similar result. For this recipe, it's important to use an early-harvest, high-quality olive oil, which the new wave of boutique producers along the Dalmatian coast are making lots of nowadays. The herbaceousness and intensity of this style of oil work beautifully with the chariness of the calamari.

To make the wood-grilled calamari, clean the calamari by removing the tentacles from the body and, using a knife, remove the hard beak from the center of the head and reserve. With your fingers, pull the back bone, ink sac, and intestines out of the body, then peel the outer membrane/skin from the calamari and wash under cold running water.

Lay the calamari tubes on a chopping board and score with a sharp knife at ¾ inch (2 cm) intervals. Turn the tubes over and repeat.

Place the calamari, including the reserved tentacles, in a bowl with the olive oil and garlic and marinate for 4 hours.

To make the red pepper mayonnaise, place the peppers on a preheated grill and cook on all sides until the outer skin turns completely black. Place in a bowl, cover with plastic wrap, and leave to cool. Scrape off the blackened skin, cut the peppers in half, and remove the stalk and seeds. Do not wash with water or you will wash away the flavor.

Using a food processor, blend the mayonnaise and peppers and season with salt and pepper.

Preheat your grill to high heat. Remove the calamari from the marinade and drain well. Season with salt and pepper and grill over high heat for 1 minute. Turn over and cook again for 1 minute. Transfer to a serving plate.

To make the parsley and onion salad, toss together the parsley leaves, red onion, oil, and lemon juice. Season with salt and pepper and toss again.

Scatter the salad over the calamari and serve with the red pepper mayonnaise.

—Serves 6

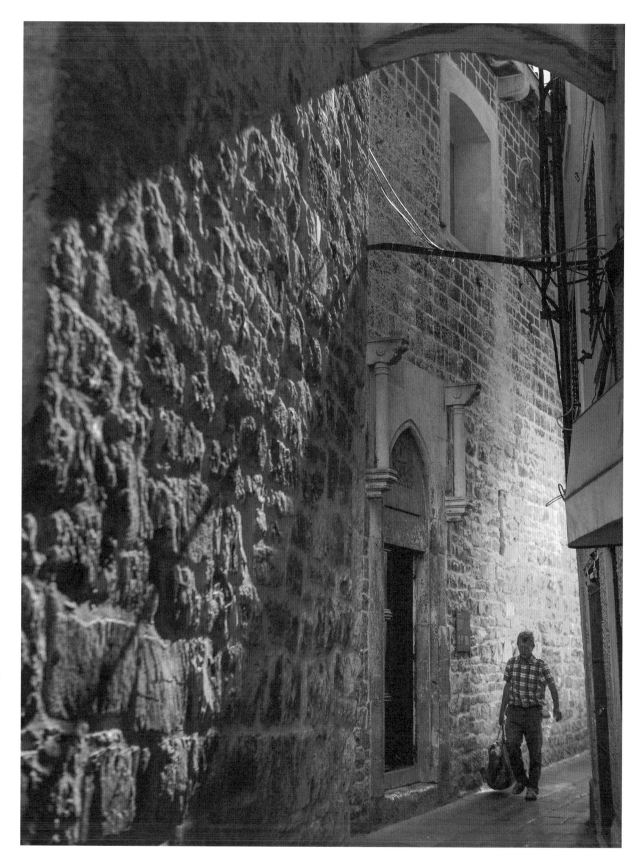

SIBENIK SALT COD FRITTERS
with SWEET-AND-SOUR VEGETABLES

Prep Time 30 minutes, plus 48 hours for soaking salt cod and marinating vegetables
Cooking Time 3 hours 10 minutes

Sweet-and-sour vegetables
2 tablespoons extra virgin olive oil
2 cups (8 oz/230 g) finely diced
   vegetables: French shallots,
   celery, bell pepper, and carrot
Generous ½ cup (150 ml) white
   wine vinegar
½ cup (3½ oz/100 g) sugar
1 bay leaf
4 black peppercorns

Salt cod fritters
9 oz (250 g) salt cod (*baccala*)
1 onion, roughly chopped
Milk, to cover the cod
14 oz (400 g) potatoes, unpeeled
2 garlic cloves, minced
1 teaspoon baking powder
½ cup (⅓ oz/10 g) parsley,
   chopped
1 egg
Generous ¾ cup (3½ oz/100 g)
   all-purpose flour
2 cups (500 ml) quality
   vegetable or olive oil, for frying
Sea salt and freshly ground
   black pepper

This is a dish inspired by an amazing meal I had at the Michelin-starred restaurant, Pelegrini, in Sibenik, arguably Croatia's best. Salt cod is commonly eaten in this part of the world, as it is throughout the rest of the Venetian Republic's territories. Traditionally served as *cicchetti* (snacks) in a whipped form on crostini or in sandwiches, these little bites are another great option for an *aperitivo*, with the sourness of the vegetables contrasting beautifully with the fritters.

To make the sweet-and-sour vegetables, place a large frying pan over medium heat, add the olive oil, and heat for 1 minute. Add the diced vegetables and sauté for 1 minute. Transfer the vegetables to a bowl.

Place the vinegar, sugar, bay leaf, and peppercorns in a small pan and bring to a boil, then pour over the diced vegetables. Leave the vegetables to marinate for at least 24 hours before serving.

To make the salt cod fritters, wash the excess salt from the cod and then soak it in cold water in the fridge for 48 hours, changing the water twice each day. This will remove most of the fish's saltiness. After 48 hours, remove the fish from the water, discard the skin, and pat dry with paper towels.

Place the cod and onion in a saucepan, cover with milk, and simmer over medium heat for 3 hours. Leave until cool enough to handle, then remove all the cod flesh from the bone and discard the onion.

Meanwhile, place the potatoes in a large saucepan, cover with cold water, and cook over low heat until tender. When the potatoes are cool enough to handle, remove the skins and coarsely mash with a potato ricer.

Combine the cooked potatoes, cod, garlic, baking powder, parsley, and egg in a bowl and season with salt and pepper. Sift in the flour and mix through evenly.

Beat the mixture well, then form into small ¾ oz (20 g) balls and refrigerate for 2 hours to set.

In a deep pan, heat the vegetable oil over medium heat to 350°F (180°C).

In small batches, fry the cod fritters for 3–4 minutes until golden brown, then remove and drain on paper towels.

To serve, place the marinated vegetables on a plate and top with the hot fritters.

—Serves 4

DALMATIAN PAN-FRIED SARDINES
with WILD HERBS AND LEMON

Prep Time 10 minutes
Cooking Time 15 minutes

1¼ cup (5½ oz/150 g) all-purpose flour
1 tablespoon lemon zest
12 sardines, scaled, gutted, and cleaned
Generous 1½ cups (375 ml) olive oil, for frying
½ cup (⅛ oz/5 g) dill
½ cup (¼ oz/8 g) marjoram
½ cup (⅛ oz/5 g) wild fennel fronds (or fennel herb fronds or bulb fennel tops)
½ cup (¼ oz/8 g) wild oregano
Scant ¼ cup (50 ml) lemon juice
Generous ½ cup (150 ml) premium Istrian extra virgin olive oil (or any quality extra virgin olive oil)
1 lemon, cut into wedges
Sea salt and freshly ground black pepper

One of my most treasured memories is being at my Zia Angela's house in the hills just outside of Toulon, France, eating freshly delivered sardines on the back of the local fish vendor's *camion* (truck). I was in my early twenties, and ever since I've absolutely loved sardines. This is a wonderfully simple dish that you will find all over the Mediterranean, and the Croatians do it as beautifully as anyone, including my aunty. If you find small enough sardines, eat them whole; if they're larger, once served, cut off the head and the back bone will come out easily.

Mix the flour and lemon zest in a large mixing bowl. Season with salt and pepper.

Place the sardines in the seasoned flour and coat lightly.

Pour approximately ½ inch (1 cm) olive oil into a large frying pan. Place over medium heat for 2 minutes, then add the sardines and cook for 2 minutes on each side.

Pick the leaves off the herbs and toss in a large bowl with the lemon juice, extra virgin olive oil, and a pinch of sea salt.

Place the sardines on a serving platter and scatter the herb salad over the top. Serve with lemon wedges.

—Serves 4

DALMATIAN SMOKED PROSCIUTTO *with* PAG SHEEP'S MILK CHEESE, BLACK OLIVES, AND CORNICHONS

Prep Time 10 minutes

5½ oz (160 g) Pag sheep's milk cheese (or Tuscan or Sardinian pecorino)
12 thin slices premium smoked prosciutto
½ cup (2½ oz/70 g) dried black olives
½ cup (2 oz/60 g) cornichons
Crusty wood-fired bread, sliced
2 tablespoons extra virgin olive oil (optional)

Pag cheese—a hard, distinctively flavored, sheep's milk cheese—is made on the Croatian island of the same name. It is one of the best pecorinos I've ever tasted and it marries wonderfully with Dris prosciutto, which is made distinctively Dalmatian by the fact that it's smoked. As well as a lovely smoky flavor, for this recipe you want prosciutto with a heavy marbling score. The additional fat content makes a big difference here and is offset beautifully by the acidity of the cornichons.

Crumble the cheese into large triangles.

Serve the cheese, prosciutto, olives, and cornichons on a platter with crusty wood-fired bread. Drizzle extra virgin olive oil over the top, if desired.

—Serves 4

VENETIAN CROATIA ✳ *Antipasti*

Pasta, rice, and pies

CLASSIC SQUID INK RISOTTO *with* GRILLED BOTTLE SQUID

Prep Time 15 minutes
Cooking Time 30 minutes

1 lb 5 oz (600 g) bottle squid, left whole (or small whole calamari)
⅔ cup (170 ml) extra virgin olive oil, plus extra for drizzling
2 white onions, finely diced
3 garlic cloves, crushed
1¾ cups (12½ oz/350 g) Vialone Nano rice (or any risotto rice)
½ cup (125 ml) white wine
2 tomatoes, chopped
4 tablespoons (2 oz/60 g) butter, softened
3 tablespoons squid ink
1 cup (2 oz/60 g) chopped parsley
4 cups (1 liter) Fish Stock (page 236)
Sea salt and freshly ground black pepper

After *pašticada*, squid ink risotto could easily take the title of Croatia's national dish and—unsurprisingly—it has a similar reputation in Venice. While the fisherman of the coast and local cooks in Croatia are adept at removing ink sacs from cuttlefish, if you want to avoid the jarred product (which is a suitable alternative), it will require quite a bit of skill and effort—and more than likely, substantial cleanup. Either way, only work with super-fresh squid.

Clean the squid by removing the head from the body, cut the beak out of the center of the head, and reserve the head and tentacles. Pull the spine, intestines, and ink sac carefully out of the body, then remove the wings and outer skin.

Heat the olive oil in a saucepan over low heat. Add the onion and garlic and cook until the onion is translucent.

Add the rice and cook for 2 minutes, then add 7 oz (200 g) of the squid. Add the wine and tomatoes and cook for 2 minutes over high heat. Stir in the butter, then stir in the squid ink and parsley.

Meanwhile, bring the stock to a boil in another pan, then reduce the heat and keep at a simmer.

Slowly add the hot fish stock to the rice, one ladle at a time, stirring continuously as the rice absorbs the stock before adding the next ladle. Cook for about 15–20 minutes until the rice is al dente. Season with salt and pepper.

Heat a cast-iron skillet over high heat until extremely hot, then sear the remaining squid tubes and tentacles quickly on both sides. Season with salt and pepper.

Spoon the risotto onto serving plates and top with the seared squid and a little more extra virgin olive oil, to taste.

—Serves 4

SWEET PEA RISOTTO

Prep Time 15 minutes
Cooking Time 30 minutes

5½ oz (160 g) smoked pancetta
⅓ cup (80 ml) extra virgin olive oil, plus extra for drizzling
2 white onions, finely diced
2 garlic cloves, sliced
1¾ cups (12½ oz/350 g) Vialone Nano rice (or any risotto rice)
1 cup (250 ml) Istrian Malvasia white wine (or any quality dry white wine)
4 cups (1 liter) Vegetable or Chicken Stock (pages 236–7)
10½ oz (300 g) sweet peas, half left whole, half puréed to a smooth paste
½ cup (1 oz/30 g) chopped parsley
2 tablespoons (1 oz/30 g) butter
½ cup (2 oz/60 g) grated Parmigiano Reggiano, plus extra to serve
Sea salt and freshly ground white pepper

This is one of Venice's most iconic dishes. But, as with *pašticada* and squid ink risotto, *rizi bizi* or sweet pea risotto, is also ubiquitous in Croatia. This recipe includes a unique Dalmatian component: crisp smoked pancetta laid over the top, delivering a beautiful salty, smoky crunch.

Preheat the oven to 350°F (180°C).

Finely dice half the pancetta and cut the remainder into thin ribbons. Place the ribbon slices on a baking sheet and cook in the oven until crisp.

Heat the olive oil in a saucepan. Add the onion, garlic, and diced pancetta and cook over low heat until the onion is translucent.

Add the rice to the pan and cook, stirring, for 2 minutes. Increase the heat to high, add the wine, and cook for 2 minutes or until the wine has evaporated.

Meanwhile, bring the stock to a boil in another pan, then reduce the heat and keep at a simmer.

Slowly add the hot stock to the rice, one ladle at a time, stirring continuously until it has been absorbed before adding the next ladle. Cook for about 12 minutes, then stir in the peas, pea purée, and parsley.

Cook for a further 3 minutes, then add the butter and Parmigiano Reggiano and season with salt and pepper. Stir well and leave for 3 minutes before serving, garnished with the crisp pancetta slices, a little extra Parmigiano Reggiano, and a drizzle of extra virgin olive oil.

—*Serves 4*

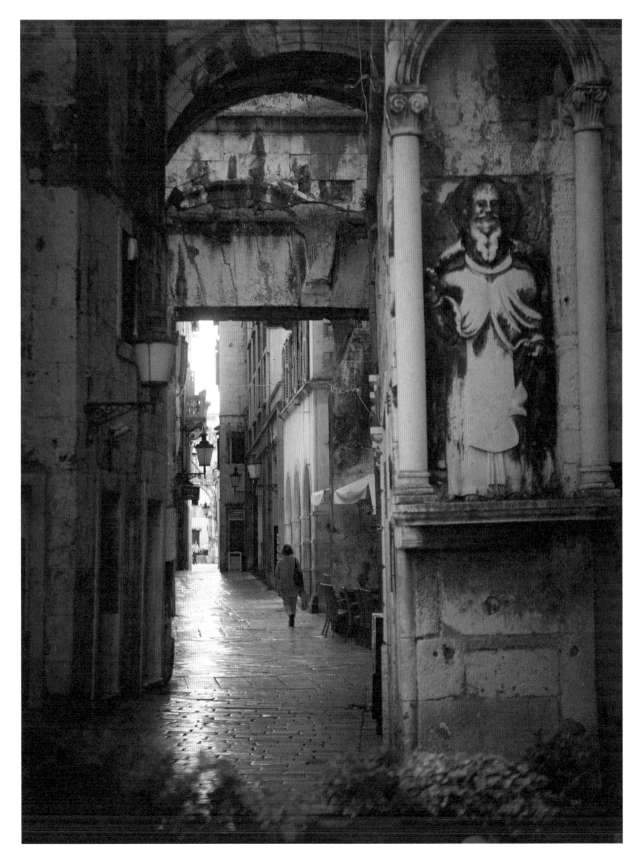

DALMATIAN PASTA AND BORLOTTI BEANS
with SMOKED PORK HOCK AND OLIVE OIL

Prep Time 30 minutes, plus overnight refrigeration of the beans
Cooking Time 1 hour 10 minutes

2 cups (14 oz/400 g) dried borlotti beans
½ cup (125 ml) extra virgin olive oil, plus extra for drizzling
5½ oz (150 g) smoked pancetta, diced into ¼ inch (5 mm) square pieces
½ cup (2½ oz/70 g) diced celery
½ cup (3 oz/80 g) diced carrot
½ cup (3 oz/80 g) finely diced onion
3 garlic cloves, crushed
1 teaspoon chopped thyme
2 potatoes, diced
7 oz (200 g) smoked ham hock or smoked pork ribs
8½ cups (2 liters) Chicken Stock (page 236)
5¼ oz (150 g) dried short pasta (macaroni)
½ cup (1 oz/30 g) chopped parsley
Grated Pag cheese (or Parmigiano Reggiano), to serve
Sea salt and freshly ground black pepper

Known locally as *pasta fazol*, this is similar to the Italian version, *pasta e fagioli*, meaning pasta and beans, found not only in Venice but throughout the whole of Italy. It's a very classic Italian dish. This version is slightly different, but equally fantastic. I love the smokiness of the hock/ribs as well as the pancetta—ingredients and flavors that are truly well mastered along the Dalmatian coast.

Place the borlotti beans in a saucepan, cover with water, and bring to a boil. Boil for 3 minutes, then cool, drain, and cover with fresh water. Refrigerate the beans overnight.

Heat the oil in a large deep saucepan over medium heat for 1 minute. Add the pancetta, celery, carrot, onion, garlic, and thyme and cook for 5 minutes, stirring continuously.

Add the drained beans, potato, ham hock, and stock and bring to a boil, then turn down the heat and cook for 1 hour, or until the beans are tender.

Take the hock out of the pan and remove the meat from the bone. Shred and return the meat to the pan along with the pasta. Cook over medium heat until the pasta is cooked. Stir in the parsley and season to taste.

Serve in pasta bowls, drizzled with olive oil and grated Pag cheese, to taste.

—Serves 10

GNOCCHI *with* ISTRIAN PORCINI MUSHROOMS *and* PAG CHEESE

Prep Time 30 minutes
Cooking Time 30 minutes

Gnocchi
1 lb 2 oz (500 g) starchy potatoes, left whole and unpeeled
1 egg, lightly beaten
Scant ½ cup (1½ oz/40 g) grated Parmigiano Reggiano
3 tablespoons (1½ oz/40 g) salted butter, softened and diced
½ teaspoon sea salt
Generous ¾ cup (3½ oz/100 g) all-purpose flour, plus extra for dusting

Sauce
½ cup (125 ml) extra virgin olive oil
11½ oz (320 g) fresh porcini mushrooms, sliced
½ tablespoon finely chopped thyme
½ cup (125 ml) white wine
⅓ cup (¾ oz/20 g) chopped parsley, plus extra to garnish
4 tablespoons grated Pag cheese (or any quality Tuscan or Sardinian pecorino), to serve
Sea salt and freshly ground black pepper

This recipe—that of my dear Croatian friend and fellow chef, Ino Kuvacic—utilizes two of my favorite ingredients: amazing porcini mushrooms, in this case grown in Istria (which borders Italy), and Pag cheese. The latter can be substituted with Parmesan or a mild pecorino. Regardless of which cheese you choose, ensure it's of a reasonable age so it can impart a beautiful, strong flavor to the finished dish. And, as with all gnocchi, moisture is your enemy here. Be sure to use very starchy potatoes, and remove as much water from them as possible after boiling by patting with dish towels. This will significantly reduce your reliance on flour, therefore guaranteeing lovely, light, and pillowy homemade gnocchi.

To make the gnocchi, place the whole potatoes in a large pan of cold water and cook over medium heat until tender.

Drain and pat-dry, then peel the potatoes while still hot. Using a food mill or mouli, purée the potatoes into a large bowl. Add the egg, Parmigiano Reggiano, butter, and sea salt, then carefully work in the flour to form a dough.

Dust a work surface with a little flour to prevent the dough sticking, then divide the dough into quarters. Roll each one into a thin log, then cut into ¾ inch (2 cm) pieces. Using a spatula, place the gnocchi on a tray lined with baking paper and refrigerate until needed.

To make the sauce, heat the oil in a large sauté pan over medium heat for 1 minute. Add the porcini mushrooms and thyme and sauté until the mushrooms have softened.

Add the white wine and parsley, increase the heat to high, and cook for 2 minutes, then season with salt and pepper.

Bring a pot of water to a boil, add the gnocchi, and cook until they rise to the surface. Drain the gnocchi, toss with the porcini sauce, and season with salt and pepper.

Finely grate the Pag cheese over the top of the gnocchi and garnish with parsley leaves before serving.

—*Serves 4*

PLJUKANCI PASTA *with* PORK AND GRAŠEVINA RAGU, ZADAR PROSCIUTTO, *and* BLACK TRUFFLES

Prep Time 40 minutes
Cooking Time 1 hour 40 minutes

14 oz (400 g) Fresh Egg
  Pasta Dough (page 240)
4 tablespoons extra virgin
  olive oil
1 lb 5 oz (600 g) ground pork
  (30% fat)
1 onion, finely sliced
½ cup (3 oz/80 g) finely diced
  carrot
½ cup (2½ oz/70 g) finely diced
  celery
4 garlic cloves, chopped
1 cup (250 ml) Graševina white
  wine (or any good-quality dry
  white wine)
2 cups (500 ml) Chicken Stock
  (page 236)
1 tablespoon chopped rosemary
2 bay leaves
6 thin slices Zadar prosciutto
  (or any high-quality prosciutto)
1½ oz (40 g) Zadar black truffle
  (or any black truffle)
Pag cheese or Parmigiano
  Reggiano, to serve (optional)
Sea salt and freshly ground
  black pepper

Making use of local truffles from Rovijn, this dish is very similar to what's served throughout Northern Italy but, once again, has the distinctive smoky aroma and taste of local prosciutto. Pljukanci, a hand-rolled, spindle-shaped pasta that hails from the Croatian region of Istria, is easier to make than you'd think, and an absolute joy to eat.

Take small, nut-sized pieces of pasta dough and roll between the palms of your hands to create long, thin noodles, similar in size to green beans, but thinner at the ends. Place the pasta on a lightly floured tray.

Heat 2 tablespoons of the olive oil in a pan over high heat for 2 minutes, then add the ground pork and cook until browned. Remove the pork from the pan and set aside.

Add the remaining 2 tablespoons olive oil to the pan, add the onion, carrot, celery, and garlic, and cook over low heat until the onion is translucent.

Return the pork, with any juices, to the pan, add the white wine, and cook over high heat for 2 minutes.

Add the chicken stock, rosemary, and bay leaves to the pan and cook over low heat for 90 minutes.

Cut the prosciutto into thin strips and fold through the pork ragu. Season with salt and pepper.

Place the pasta into a large pot of boiling salted water and cook for just 2 minutes. Drain the pasta and toss through the pork ragu.

Shave or grate the truffle over the top of the pasta before serving. You can also add grated Pag or Parmigiano, if desired.

—Serves 6

SPINACH AND NETTLE RISOTTO *with* SEA SCALLOPS

Prep Time 30 minutes
Cooking Time 45 minutes

3½ oz (100 g) stinging nettles
   (or spinach)
3½ oz (100 g) spinach
⅓ cup (70 ml) olive oil
1 onion, finely diced
1¾ cups (12½ oz/350 g) Vialone
   Nano rice (or any risotto rice)
½ cup (125 ml) white wine
6⅓ cups (1.5 liters) Vegetable or
   Chicken Stock (pages 236–7)
7 tablespoons (3½ oz/100 g)
   butter
12 half-shell scallops
1 garlic clove, minced
Sea salt and freshly ground
   black pepper

The visual wow factor here is thanks to the vibrant green of the nettles, best picked in early spring. Of course, you don't need to serve the scallops in their shells, but they not only add to the dish's aesthetic appeal, they also allow the scallops—which should be only just caramelized on both sides—to sit in the beautiful garlic butter.

Wear food prep gloves to prepare the stinging nettles. Pick the nettle leaves from their stalks and place in a bowl of cold water.

Bring a large pot of salted water to a boil. Place the nettles and spinach in the boiling water for approximately 30 seconds until just wilted. Remove from the water and place in a bowl of ice water to stop the cooking process.

Drain the spinach and nettles and squeeze to remove any water. Process in a food processor to a smooth purée, adding a little cold water or stock, if needed.

Heat the olive oil in a saucepan, add the onion, and cook over low heat until translucent. Add the rice and cook for 2 minutes, stirring continuously. Add the white wine and cook for 2 minutes.

Meanwhile, bring the stock to a boil in another pan, then reduce the heat and keep at a simmer.

Slowly add the hot stock to the rice, one ladle at a time, stirring continuously as the rice absorbs the stock between each addition. Cook for 15–20 minutes. Season with salt and pepper.

Fold the spinach and nettle purée into the risotto. Add half the butter and season with salt and pepper as necessary, then stir through the risotto. Cover and set aside to rest.

Remove the scallop meat from the shells, reserving 4 shells for serving. Heat the 4 presentation shells in the oven or in boiling water.

Place a cast-iron skillet over high heat until extremely hot then sear the scallops on each side for 10 seconds. Season with salt and pepper.

Remove the scallops from the pan and add the garlic. Cook for up to 20 seconds until the garlic starts to turn golden, then add the remaining butter. Remove the pan from the heat and allow the butter to melt.

Place the risotto in serving bowls and add one scallop shell to each. Arrange three scallops in each shell. Spoon the melted butter and garlic over the scallops.

Note
Stinging nettles can be sourced from produce markets or gourmet food stores, or you can substitute more spinach.

—Serves 4

VENETIAN CROATIA ✳ *Pasta, rice, and pies*

WHOLE FLOUNDER AND HERB BREADCRUMBS
with CROATIAN SAMPHIRE

Prep Time 15 minutes
Cooking Time 1 hour

Roast potatoes
14 oz (400 g) potatoes
Generous ¾ cup (200 ml)
    extra virgin olive oil
3 tablespoons chopped rosemary
Sea salt and freshly ground
    black pepper

Flounder with herb crust
1 cup (2 oz/60 g) fresh sourdough
    breadcrumbs
1 heaped teaspoon lemon zest
Juice of 1 lemon
½ cup (⅓ oz/10 g) parsley leaves
1 × 2 lb 4 oz (1 kg) flounder,
    cleaned, scaled, and left whole
Extra virgin olive oil, to drizzle
1 lemon, cut into quarters

Croatian samphire
3 oz (80 g) samphire
    (or any sea succulent)
1 tablespoon lemon juice
3 tablespoons extra virgin olive oil

Samphire is a sea succulent that's becoming more and more popular in Europe, particularly in the Mediterranean and along the Dalmatian coast, where it's known as *motar*. It might be hard to track down, but it's worth the effort: it adds a lovely fresh, salty element to the fish, and matches perfectly with the potatoes (make sure you get them crisp) and the fish's herb crust.

Preheat the oven to 350°F (180°C).

To make the roast potatoes, finely slice the potatoes ¼ inch (5 mm) thick and toss in the extra virgin olive oil. Add the chopped rosemary and season with salt and pepper.

Layer the potatoes, overlapping them slightly to cover the base of a large ovensafe dish. Roast in the oven for 25 minutes, until browned and crisp. Remove and cover with foil. Increase the oven to 400°F (200°C).

To make the flounder with herb crust, place the breadcrumbs, lemon zest, lemon juice, and parsley in a food processor and blend until the crumbs become bright green. Season with salt and pepper.

Season the flounder with salt and pepper on each side and in the internal cavity. Place on a paper-lined baking sheet and drizzle with extra virgin olive oil. Lightly and evenly cover the flounder with the herb crust.

Bake the flounder for 25–30 minutes or until just cooked. Just before the fish is ready, return the potatoes to the oven to reheat.

Meanwhile, to make the Croatian samphire, place the samphire in a pan of boiling salted water for 20 seconds, then drain and toss with the lemon juice and extra virgin olive oil. Season with sea salt and pepper.

Serve the flounder with the roasted potatoes, samphire, and lemon quarters.

—Serves 4

CLASSIC DALMATIAN COAST SEAFOOD GRILL

Prep Time 20 minutes
Cooking Time 1 hour 45 minutes

1 × 10½ oz (300 g) octopus
1 × 1 lb 2 oz (500 g) snapper,
    cleaned, scaled, and left whole
4 large shrimp, cut
    in half and left in shells
4 scampi/langoustines (or large
    shrimp), cut in half and left in
    shells
1 cup (250 ml) extra virgin olive
    oil, plus extra for the lemon
    and to drizzle
1 lemon, cut in half
Wild herbs, to garnish
Sea salt and freshly ground
    black pepper

This is a classic example of Mediterranean cooking and can be found all along the Dalmatian coast in a form that's basically identical to what is seen in Venice. What I most love about this dish is how it allows the quality of the seafood to speak for itself. In Croatia this dish usually includes a whole fish and, in fact, there's often more than one different type. Croatians understand that eating fish on the bone really is the best way to enjoy seafood, and I couldn't agree more.

With a heavy meat mallet or rolling pin, beat the octopus for about 20 seconds to tenderize.

Place the whole octopus into a pot of salted boiling water. When the water comes back to a boil, turn the heat down to medium and cook for 90 minutes. Remove from the heat and leave to cool in the cooking liquid. Drain the octopus and cut into individual tentacles.

Preheat a grill until medium-hot.

Lightly coat the seafood with olive oil and season with salt and pepper. Place the snapper on the grill and cook on each side for approximately 6–8 minutes (the cooking time varies with the size of fish and the heat of the grill).

Five minutes before the snapper is ready, add the octopus, turning after 2 minutes. Add the shrimp and scampi: these will take about 2 minutes to cook.

Brush the cut side of each lemon half with olive oil and grill until caramelized.

Serve the grilled seafood on a platter with the lemon, drizzled with extra virgin olive oil. Garnish with any wild herbs.

—Serves 4

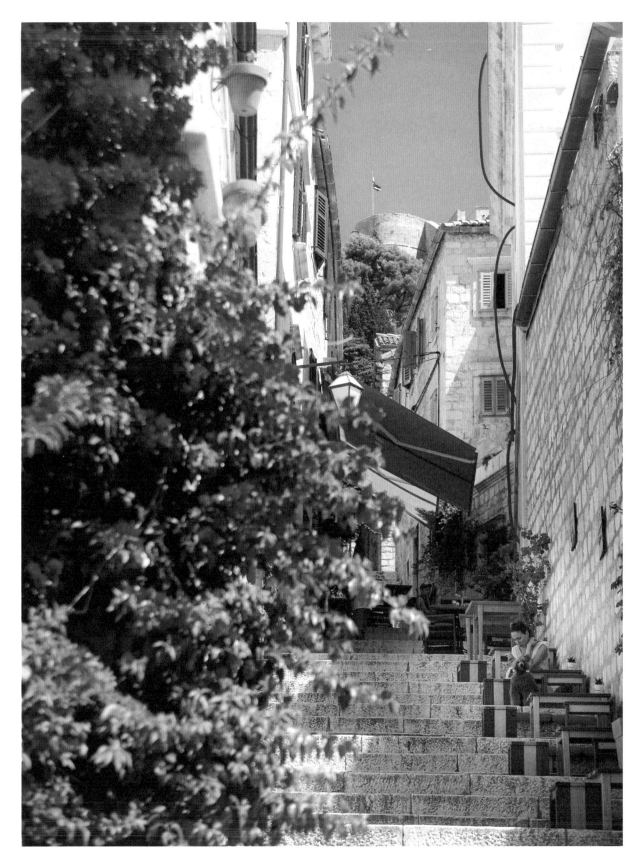

DUBROVNIK TUNA PAŠTICADA
with YELLOW POLENTA *and* SMOKED EGGPLANT

Prep Time 15 minutes
Cooking Time 45 minutes

Red wine sauce
Scant ½ cup (100 ml) extra
    virgin olive oil
2 cups (11 oz/310 g) finely diced
    onion
4 garlic cloves, crushed
1¼ cups (300 ml) Plavac Mali red
    wine (or Primitivo or Zinfandel)
Scant ¼ cup (50 ml) Prošek sweet
    wine (or any quality white
    dessert wine)
2 oz (60 g) dates, diced

Grilled polenta
1 teaspoon sea salt
⅔ cup (4½ oz/125 g) fine yellow
    polenta cornmeal
⅔ cup (2 oz/60 g) finely
    grated Parmigiano Reggiano

Smoked eggplant
1 eggplant
⅓ cup (¾ oz/20 g) chopped
    parsley
4 tablespoons extra virgin olive oil
1 tablespoon red wine vinegar
1 garlic clove, finely diced
Sea salt and freshly ground
    black pepper

Tuna steak
1 lb 7 oz (640 g) tuna loin, cut
    into 4 steaks
2 tablespoons olive oil

This is quite a modern interpretation of *pašticada*, which as I've said is one of Croatia's national dishes. And, while it's clearly different to Venice's version, which showcases beef, the two key similarities are the red wine—in this case Croatia's celebrated Plavac Mali—and the inclusion of polenta, used in various forms and guises throughout the region, but which should be nice and crispy here.

To make the red wine sauce, heat the olive oil and onion in a saucepan over low heat and cook, stirring continuously, until the onion is translucent. Add the garlic and cook for 2 minutes.

Add both the wines to the pan and cook until reduced to a third of the original volume. Stir in the dates and set aside to cool.

To make the polenta, place 2 cups (500 ml) water and the salt into a saucepan and bring to a boil. Pour the polenta into the water in a slow, steady stream, stirring continuously. Turn the heat to low and cook, stirring, for 20 minutes.

Grease a small baking tray. Stir the Parmigiano Reggiano into the polenta. Pour the polenta into the greased tray and leave to cool: the polenta should be approximately 1¼ inches (3 cm) thick. When cool, cut the polenta into 2 inch (5 cm) squares.

To make the smoked eggplant, preheat your grill or broiler until hot and cook the eggplant until the skin is completely charred all over. Put the eggplant in a bowl, cover with plastic wrap, and leave to cool.

When cool enough to handle, carefully cut the eggplant in half and scoop out the flesh with a spoon. Place the eggplant flesh in a clean bowl and fold in the parsley, olive oil, red wine vinegar, and garlic. Season with salt and pepper.

Preheat a grill pan or cast-iron skillet over high heat.

Lightly brush the tuna steaks with olive oil and season with salt on both sides. Cook the tuna and polenta squares on the grill for 2 minutes on each side.

Arrange the polenta on serving plates and top with smoked eggplant and the tuna steaks. Spoon the red wine sauce over the fish before serving.

—Serves 4

ISTRIAN MIXED SHELLFISH BUZARU

Prep Time 15 minutes
Cooking Time 20 minutes

Generous ¾ cup (200 ml) Istrian extra virgin olive oil (or any quality extra virgin olive oil), plus extra for drizzling
4 tablespoons fresh breadcrumbs
4 garlic cloves, finely chopped
12½ oz (350 g) peeled shrimp
12½ oz (350 g) lobster tail, shell on, cut into 4 escalope pieces
12½ oz (350 g) whole scampi/ langoustines (or large shrimp)
12½ oz (350 g) venus clams
1½ cups (375 ml) Malvasia white wine (or any quality medium– dry white wine)
5 oz (140 g) quality tomato passata (puréed tomatoes)
1 tablespoon chopped parsley
Crusty bread, to serve
Sea salt and freshly ground black pepper

Known throughout the Croatian coast as *buzaru*, the classic version of this dish calls only for scampi, served in a simple but delightful tomato sauce. The recipe is also common in Venice and the Veneto, but it's usually accompanied by pasta—primarily spaghetti. Both versions are absolutely delicious, but I have to say I love this recipe, with its wider range of fish and shellfish.

Heat a scant ½ cup (100 ml) extra virgin olive oil in a small frying pan over medium heat for 1 minute, then add the breadcrumbs and fry until golden brown. Drain on paper towels.

Heat the remaining olive oil in a saucepan, add the garlic, and cook gently over low heat for 2 minutes, taking care it doesn't brown. Add the shellfish and wine and cook until the scampi and lobster start to become pink.

Add the tomato passata and cook for 5 minutes until the sauce thickens. Season with salt and pepper and stir in the parsley.

Serve on a deep platter, sprinkled with the fried breadcrumbs and drizzled with a little extra virgin olive, to taste. Serve with crusty bread.

—Serves 4

BRAISED PAG LAMB SHOULDER *with* OLIVE OIL MASHED POTATOES *and* GRILLED BABY LEEKS

Prep Time 10 minutes
Cooking Time 4 hours 15 minutes

Lamb shoulder
1 × 2 lb 10 oz (1.2 kg) lamb shoulder
2 tablespoons olive oil
1 cup (4 oz/120 g) whole
  French shallots
5 garlic cloves, crushed
1 bottle Plavac Mali red wine
  (or Zinfandel, Primitivo, or
  any medium/full-bodied
  red wine)
½ cup (125 ml) red wine vinegar
1 sprig thyme
1 sprig rosemary
2 bay leaves
Sea salt and freshly ground
  black pepper

Olive oil mashed potatoes
1 lb 12 oz (800 g) potatoes, left
  whole and unpeeled
Generous ¾ cup (200 ml) olive oil

Grilled baby leeks
20 baby leeks
3 tablespoons extra virgin olive oil

The wonderful Croatian island of Pag, best known for its eponymous sheep's milk cheese, also (and unsurprisingly) produces absolutely stunning lamb. This is a great winter dish, with the meat falling off the bone and packing a flavorful punch, thanks to both the hint of acidity from the vinegar and the richness of the Plavac Mali, the superstar red wine of the Croatian islands.

Preheat the oven to 315°F (160°C).

Season the lamb shoulder well with salt and pepper.

Heat the olive oil in a large, deep Dutch oven over high heat for 2 minutes. Carefully add the lamb shoulder and brown all over. Remove the lamb and set aside.

Turn the heat to low, add the shallots and garlic, and cook until softened.

Return the lamb to the pot and cover with the red wine and vinegar. Add the thyme, rosemary, and bay leaves. Cover and cook in the oven for 3½ hours or until the lamb is very tender.

Remove the lamb, cover with foil, and set aside in a warm place. Pass the liquid through a fine sieve and return the cooking juices to a saucepan over low heat. Simmer the liquid until it reduces to a sauce consistency, then keep warm.

Meanwhile, to make the olive oil mashed potatoes, place the whole potatoes in a large deep pot of cold water and boil until cooked through. While still hot, peel the potatoes and purée in a food mill or mouli. Beat in the oil and season with salt.

To make the grilled baby leeks, trim the roots off the leeks, brush with olive oil, and season with salt. Place on a hot grill or grill pan and cook for 1 minute on each side.

Serve the lamb on a platter with the sauce, olive oil mashed potatoes, and baby leeks.

—Serves 4

SPIT-ROASTED CHICKEN AND WHITE ROVINJ TRUFFLE *with* POTATO AND RAINBOW CHARD

Prep Time 15 minutes
Cooking Time 1 hour

Spit-roasted chicken
1 medium stewing chicken
10½ tablespoons (5½ oz/150 g) butter, softened
¼ cup (60 ml) extra virgin olive oil
1 whole head of garlic
¼ cup (⅙ oz/5 g) thyme leaves
¾ oz (20 g) Rovinj truffle (or any white or black truffle—black truffles have a milder flavor)
Sea salt and freshly ground black pepper

Potato and rainbow chard
3 potatoes, peeled, cut into 1 inch (2.5 cm) dice
⅓ cup (80 ml) extra virgin olive oil
4 garlic cloves, finely sliced
1 bunch orange and red chard, cut into ¾ inch (2 cm) strips

Croatians enjoy cooking and eating meat and fish on the bone, and this dish is a stunning example. Spit-roasting the chicken keeps the flesh lovely and moist, while also giving it a wonderfully caramelized skin. If you're not able to use a spit, oven roasting will work well too, although you might miss the lovely charred flavor that comes from cooking over a flame. For those who can find (and afford) such a luxury, the truffle makes a sensational addition, as does the potato and rainbow chard—a classic combination seen all over the Croatian coast.

For the spit-roasted chicken, preheat the spit roast to a medium–high heat, or the oven to 350°F (180°C).

Starting at the neck end of the bird, use your finger to separate the skin from the flesh, pushing your hand between the skin and breast meat to form a cavity, then gently do the same to the thighs, making sure not to tear the skin.

Spread the softened butter evenly in the cavity under the skin. Rub the olive oil all over the bird, then season with salt and pepper inside and out. Cut the head of garlic in half and place inside the bird with the thyme. Place the bird onto the spit and secure according to the manufacturer's instructions.

Cook until the bird's internal temperature reaches 160°F (70°C)—this should take approximately 1 hour. Alternatively, roast in the oven for 50–60 minutes. Then cover with foil and leave to rest for 20 minutes.

Meanwhile, make the potato and rainbow chard. Put the potato in a pot of cold water and boil over high heat until tender but not falling apart. Drain.

Place a large frying pan over low heat, add the olive oil and garlic, and cook for 2 minutes. Add the potatoes and cook for 3–4 minutes. Add the chard and cook until wilted. Season with salt and pepper.

Carve the bird using a sharp knife: remove the legs, then the breast meat, cut into even pieces, and arrange on a serving platter.

Slice or grate the truffle over the bird and serve with the potato and rainbow chard.

—Serves 4

Dolci

CROATIAN BLACKBERRY CRUMBLE

Prep Time 15 minutes
Cooking Time 50 minutes

Pastry
1¼ cup (5½ oz/150 g) all-purpose
    flour
⅓ teaspoon baking powder
12 tablespoons (6 oz/170 g) cold
    butter, diced
½ cup (4 oz/110 g) sugar
2 egg yolks

Blackberry filling
2 egg whites
½ cup (4 oz/110 g) sugar
1 lb 2 oz (500 g) blackberries
Seeds from ½ vanilla bean
1 teaspoon lemon zest

1 tablespoon confectioners' sugar,
    for dusting

In many parts of the world, fruit crumble desserts like this one are reserved for the cold of winter. Not in this case, as blackberries are at their best in summer, and this Croatian staple—another example of Slavic influence on the Dalmatian coast— is beautifully light and fantastic for summer.

Preheat the oven to 350°F (180°C).

To make the pastry, mix the flour, baking powder, butter, sugar, and egg yolks in a food processor until a dough ball forms. Turn out of the processor and set aside one-third of the dough to make the topping.

Grease an 8 inch (20 cm) pie dish and firmly press the dough into the base and sides of the dish to form a crust.

For the blackberry filling, whisk the egg whites and sugar to soft peaks. Fold in the berries, vanilla seeds, and lemon zest and pour into the pie dish.

Crumble the reserved pastry dough over the top of the blackberry filling.

Bake the crumble in the oven for about 50 minutes, or until golden.

Allow to cool a little, then dust with confectioners' sugar. This is beautiful with vanilla gelato or cream.

—Serves 8

RAB ISLAND ALMOND AND MARASCHINO LIQUEUR CAKE

Prep Time 30 minutes, plus 1 hour for resting the dough
Cooking Time 50 minutes

Dough
1 cup (4½ oz/130 g) 00 flour
1 egg, beaten
1½ tablespoons (¾ oz/20 g) unsalted butter, softened
1 tablespoon sugar
1 pinch sea salt

Filling
2 cups (7 oz/200 g) ground almonds
1⅔ cups (7 oz/200 g) confectioners' sugar, plus extra for dusting
1 egg
1 tablespoon maraschino cherry liqueur
Zest of 1 orange
Zest of 1 lemon

6 whole blanched almonds

It's said that this cake was first served to Pope Alexander III in 1177 on the Croatian island of Rab, and it became a delicacy served to the aristocracy during the Venetian Republic's dynasty. Today, it's served at festive occasions, including baptisms and weddings, and is one of the island's most famous exports. And, while the traditional spiral shape is sometimes replaced with a heart or a horseshoe, it's considered almost sacrilegious in Rab's town to deviate from the classic recipe. Resembling more of a cookie than a cake when cut, Rab cake is just beautiful served with coffee.

To make the dough, mix together the flour, egg, and butter in a large bowl. Add 2½ tablespoons water, and the sugar and salt, and knead for 12 minutes to form a smooth, silky dough.

Divide the dough in half, cover with plastic wrap, and leave to rest for 1 hour.

Preheat the oven to 250°F (120°C).

To make the filling, combine the ground almonds, confectioners' sugar, egg, liqueur, and orange and lemon zests in a large bowl and beat together with a spatula.

Place half the dough on a floured work surface and, using a rolling pin, roll out to a 10 × 12 inch (25 × 30 cm) rectangle. Place on a baking sheet lined with parchment paper.

Using a pastry wheel, cut the dough into a tight spiral snake, 2 inches (5 cm) wide, then top the pastry spiral with the filling to cover all the pastry.

Roll out the other half of the pastry dough to the same thickness as the base, and cut into ¾ inch (2 cm) wide ribbons. Attach the ribbons of dough all the way around the edges of the spiral, pinching the dough together to seal.

Score the top of the cake filling with a fork to decorate, then press the whole almonds into the top.

Bake for 50 minutes, or until the outside crust is firm. Just before serving, dust with confectioners' sugar.

—Serves 8

VENETIAN CROATIA ✳ *Dolci*

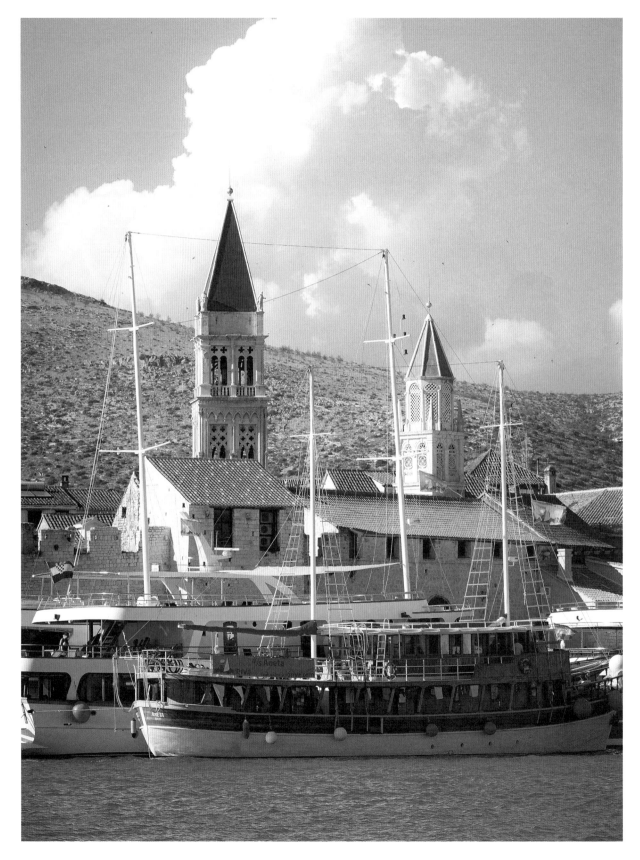

APPLE AND CHERRY STRUDEL

Prep Time 10 minutes
Cooking Time 50 minutes

1 tablespoon honey
1 lb (450 g) cooking apples
1 tablespoon lemon zest
11½ oz (325 g) pitted fresh cherries
  (12½ oz/350 g unprepared)
⅓ cup (2 oz/60 g) brown sugar
¼ teaspoon fine sea salt
1 teaspoon ground cinnamon
1¼ cups (5½ oz/150 g) walnut
  halves
10 sheets filo pastry
7 tablespoons (3½ oz/100 g)
  butter, melted
2 tablespoons sugar

Like pancakes, strudels are ubiquitous in Croatia. Served in patisseries and a regular menu inclusion along the Dalmatian coast, strudels like this one are also seen in the northern parts of the Veneto, especially in the town of Belluno and farther north near the Austrian and Slovenian borders. Cherries, a staple fruit in Croatia used in a range of desserts and liqueurs, are the star here, so make sure you find them at their peak.

Preheat the oven to 315°F (160°C).

Gently heat the honey in a pan over low heat until it becomes runny, like water.

Peel, core, and dice the apples into ½ inch (1 cm) cubes. Combine in a large mixing bowl with the honey, lemon zest, pitted cherries, brown sugar, sea salt, cinnamon, and walnuts.

Brush each sheet of filo all over with melted butter and lay the sheets on top of one another. Spoon the apple and cherry filling lengthwise onto the pastry, to about 1½ inches (4 cm) from each end of the pastry. Fold the pastry from one side and roll to form a log. Fold in the ends to seal in the filling and then brush the outside of the pastry with butter. Sprinkle with sugar.

Place the strudel on a baking sheet and bake for 35–45 minutes.

Allow to cool for 20 minutes before slicing to serve.

—*Serves 10*

DUBROVNIK ROSE LIQUEUR, RICOTTA, AND ALMOND CREPES
with CANDIED ROSE PETALS

Prep Time 10 minutes, plus overnight drying of rose petals and 20 minutes for resting batter
Cooking Time 10 minutes

Candied rose petals
3 egg whites
1 cup (¾ oz/20 g) clean, unsprayed rose petals
Generous ½ cup (4 oz/120 g) sugar

Crepe batter
1¼ cup (5½ oz/150 g) all-purpose flour, sifted
1 egg, beaten
1½ cups (375 ml) milk
2 tablespoons (1 oz/30 g) butter

Ricotta filling
1 cup (8 oz/230 g) ricotta
1 cup (8½ oz/240 g) Mascarpone, (page 243)
¼ cup (1 oz/30 g) confectioners' sugar, plus extra for dusting
3 tablespoons Dubrovnik rose liqueur (or rose water)
1 cup (5½ oz/160 g) roasted blanched almonds, chopped

Pancakes and crepes are absolutely everywhere in Croatia and, in fact, are hugely popular throughout much of Europe. Less common is the combination of ingredients I've used here; however, each one is classically Croatian and they're stunning all together. This is a simple but beautiful treat for all the senses, with the candied rose petals adding a great visual element.

To make the candied rose petals, lightly whisk the egg whites to a frothy consistency, then lightly brush the rose petals with egg whites. Dip into the sugar, then arrange the petals on a tray lined with parchment paper. Place the tray of petals in a warm dry place to dry overnight.

To make the crepes, place the flour in a large mixing bowl and make a well in middle. Add the egg and a little milk and whisk to a smooth paste. Whisk in the remaining milk. Pass through a fine sieve and leave to rest for 20 minutes.

Heat a non-stick frying pan or crepe pan over medium heat and add ½ teaspoon of the butter. Add a small ladle of crepe batter to cover the base of the pan. Cook for 1 minute, flip the crepe, and cook for another 1 minute. Repeat with the remaining crepe batter.

To make the ricotta filling, whisk together the ricotta, mascarpone, confectioners' sugar, and rose liqueur until smooth. Fold in half the chopped almonds.

Place 3 tablespoons of ricotta filling on each crepe and spread evenly. Roll each crepe into a cigar shape.

Dust the crepes with confectioners' sugar and serve with candied rose petals and the remaining chopped almonds.

—Serves 4

GREEK ISLANDS OF THE REPUBLIC

IV

GATEWAY TO THE EAST

To this day, the people of the Greek lands formerly under Venetian rule often reflect nostalgically on this part of their history. While foreign invasion was never going to be a harmonious event, Venetian rule brought stabilizing benefits to this part of the world and its people. It meant protection from the East and frequently facilitated a livelihood supported by Venice's international trade of key Greek agricultural assets. For the most part, Venice's reign over her Greek territories was mutually beneficial, with many cultural blessings being shared between the two throughout the Republic's 450-odd year rule.

Corfu, with her strategic location and rich agricultural potential, was a significant coup, forming part of the Republic in 1386. It, and a multitude of islands and land-based ports in both the Ionian and Aegean Seas, formed Venice's key Greek outposts. Zante, Cephalonia, Ithaca, Lefkada, and Kythera formed the Venetian-ruled Ionian islands: the only Greek-speaking territories (with the exception of Cephalonia for a very short period of time) that didn't succumb to Ottoman rule. Crete, Santorini, and Cyprus were key Venetian-held islands in the Aegean.

Under Venetian rule, the islands' economies were primarily based on producing and exporting trading commodities. On Corfu, the most important agricultural product was olive oil. This was also the case on Cephalonia and Zante, along with raisins and wine. For Crete, it was grain, hides, and wood for shipbuilding.

Occupying parts of Greece was extremely valuable to Venice. Just as with the Dalmatian coast, gaining control of the Greek island ports bolstered the Republic's trading capabilities in the East Mediterranean, which by the end of the 14th century had reached almost monopolistic status. Greece was the gateway between the East and West, and the authority that the Ottomans exerted on her mainland was matched by Venice in the water. Control of the Greek islands secured Venice's trading relationship with the Levant—with Crete and Cyprus of particular importance. This was key to Venice cementing her status as an economic powerhouse. And, as was the case with the Croatian coast, the Venetian raison d'etre and way of life was also ideally suited to these islands, with her boats very much at home in these waters.

Some Greeks profited enormously from this arrangement. The Greek aristocratic classes of the day, owners of large areas of Greek land, enjoyed the full fruits of these export markets. The arrangement also facilitated access to "new" and "exotic" foods introduced by Venetians from the Americas and Indies, including corn, tomatoes, beans, and coffee, commodities that have since become synonymous with daily life in Greece.

The legacy of the Venetian Republic can still be seen on the islands today, where there are numerous and clear parallels between their cuisine and that of Venice. But what I also find fascinating are the linguistic similarities between the two regions—not all that surprising considering that despite Venice's rule ending in 1797, Italian was still the official language of the Ionian islands until well into the 1800s.

The correlations are perhaps most evident in Corfu, the closest island to Italy, a kind of Venice without canals. Their classic *bourdeto* is a spicy fish stew whose name, like the Croatians' *brodet*, hails from the Italian word *brodetto*, meaning "broth." Corfiot *pastitsada* (again like Croatia's *pašticada*) also closely resembles Venice's *pastissada*, a slow-cooked beef stew, but using rooster or veal as the primary ingredient. *Bianco*, the Italian word for "white," is fish usually cooked in a lemon or white wine sauce with garlic (as it often is in Italy). A typical fish dish on many Greek islands is *savoro*—inarguably a direct relative of Venice's *in saor*. The language similarities extend beyond the culinary. The words *nonna* and *nonno* for "grandmother" and "grandfather" is a significant language difference between the Venetian-ruled territories and the rest of Greece, and a clear example of the longevity of Venice's impact in this part of the world. There are many other examples. Further, in Corfu, those with ethnic and linguistic ties to the Venetian Republic are still known as Corfiot Italians. During Venice's leadership, many Venetians moved to the Greek island, incentivized by free land. Today you'd struggle to find a more Venetian island outside of Italy. Likewise, Lefkada was settled by people from the Venetian island of Burano, who brought with them the age-old custom of charcuterie making, a custom for which Lefkada is famous to this day—and an artform noticeably absent elsewhere in Greece. Crete too was significant, and was the Republic's most important cultural center outside of Venice during this period.

Symbols of Venice's influence are scattered across many of the Greek islands. The look and feel of Ithaca's capital, Vathi, is very Venetian—even to the point that after devastating earthquakes in 1953, the Venetian buildings were rebuilt in the exact same style and, in 1978, a law was passed prohibiting repairs in any other manner. Zakynthos boasts her own Piazza San Marco, albeit a small and less revered version of the Venetian original. In Cephalonia, the Assos Castle—now a popular tourist attraction—was built in the 16th century to fend off invasion. It's the work of Venetian architect Marino Gentilini, whose descendants remained on the island and now produce some of her most stunning wines, particularly the indigenous varieties, Robola and Mavrodaphne. And what does each bottle proudly display? A logo boasting none other than a Venetian lion. In Crete, the Venetian harbor of Chania was used to manage trade and fend off pirates, and together with her lighthouse (also built by the Venetians) is probably the island's most recognized setting. Finally, in the Republic's farthest flung territory, Cyprus' fortifications and bridges are present-day reminders of the island's role as a military base, enabling its trade with the Levant.

The following recipes provide an illuminating snapshot into the cuisine of these unique islands. The Venetian influence is apparent in most of the dishes, and I think it is some of Greece's best food.

GREEK ISLANDS OF THE REPUBLIC

Antipasti

IONIAN ISLAND BRUSCHETTE

In this recipe I've used sourdough baguette, but in Greece twice-cooked barley or wheat flour rusks are commonly used. If you'd like to do the same—and can find them—be sure to sprinkle the tops of the rusks with a little water. This will soften them slightly, but leave the bases crunchy. The toppings here range from the humble *riganada* with cherry tomatoes and feta, to the more elaborate sea urchin roe, which has sadly been almost completely fished out in the Ionian islands, but is readily available in other parts of the world. Traditionally, sea urchin bruschette are served with just the roe and olive oil, but I've added beautiful crisp sage leaves coated in butter, found in abundance on the islands.

ITHACAN SEA URCHIN AND MONASTERY BREAD BRUSCHETTE

Prep Time 5 minutes
Cooking Time 5 minutes

7 tablespoons (3½ oz/100 g) salted butter
24 sage leaves
½ small monastery sourdough baguette (or any quality artisanal sourdough baguette)
6 tablespoons extra virgin olive oil
12 pieces (3½ oz/100 g) fresh sea urchin roe
Sea salt

—*Serves 6*

Heat the butter in a saucepan and cook the sage leaves over medium–high heat until golden brown and crisp. Transfer the leaves to paper towels.

Slice the bread into twelve ⅓ inch (8 mm) thick pieces. Lightly toast the bread on both sides and place on a serving platter. Drizzle with half the olive oil, then place the sea urchin roe on top. Place two crisp sage leaves on each piece, drizzle with the remaining olive oil, and garnish with salt.

Serve immediately.

RIGANADA

Prep Time 10 minutes

½ small monastery sourdough baguette (or any quality artisanal sourdough baguette)
6 tablespoons extra virgin olive oil
5½ oz (160 g) sheep's milk feta, sliced
14 oz (400 g) ripe cherry tomatoes, quartered
¼ red onion, sliced
2 tablespoons dried Greek oregano
Sea salt and freshly ground black pepper

—*Serves 6*

Slice the bread into twelve ⅓ inch (8 mm) thick pieces. Lightly toast the bread on both sides and place on a serving platter. Drizzle with a little olive oil and then top each piece with feta, cherry tomatoes, and red onion. Season with sea salt and pepper.

Drizzle with a little more olive oil, sprinkle generously with oregano, and drizzle more oil over the top to finish.

HARRY'S VEAL AND FETA BRUSCHETTE

Prep Time 10 minutes
Cooking Time 50 minutes

Generous ½ cup (150 ml) extra virgin olive oil
1 onion, finely sliced
½ cup (3 oz/80 g) finely diced carrot
½ cup (2½ oz/70 g) finely diced celery
2 garlic cloves, finely chopped
1 lb 2 oz (500 g) ground veal (30% fat)
1 cup (250 ml) white wine
1 cup (250 ml) Chicken Stock (page 236)
3 large sprigs wild island thyme (or cultivated thyme), plus extra
    to garnish
2 bay leaves
½ small monastery sourdough baguette (or any quality
    artisanal sourdough baguette)
4 oz (120 g) Greek feta cheese, crumbled
Sea salt and freshly ground black pepper

—Serves 6

Place a saucepan over high heat, add half the olive
oil, and heat for 2 minutes. Add the onion, carrot,
celery, and garlic and cook over low heat until the
onion is translucent.

Remove the vegetables from the pan. Add the remaining
olive oil to the pan, then add the veal and brown the meat
on all sides.

Return the vegetables to the pan. Add the white wine
and cook over high heat for 2 minutes.

Add the stock, thyme, and bay leaves and cook over low
heat for 30 minutes. Season with salt and pepper.

Slice the bread into twelve ⅓ inch (8 mm) thick pieces.
Lightly toast the bread on both sides and place on a
serving platter. Top with the veal, then crumble feta
cheese and extra thyme over the top.

CEPHALONIAN RAZOR CLAMS IN GENTILINI ROBOLA

Prep Time 5 minutes, plus 4 hours for soaking the clams
Cooking Time 5 minutes

2 lb 4 oz (1 kg) razor clams
½ cup (125 ml) Gentilini extra virgin olive oil (or any quality early-harvest extra virgin olive oil), plus extra to serve
4 garlic cloves, finely sliced
1 cup (250 ml) Gentilini Robola white wine (or any aromatic Riesling)
10½ oz (300 g) cherry tomatoes, cut in half
3 tablespoons chopped parsley
Sea salt and freshly ground black pepper

Razor clams would have to be one of my favorite ingredients; I eat them as often as I can when I'm in Europe. Cephalonians feel the same, and in this dish the razor clams are married with Robola wine and olive oil—both from the acclaimed producer Gentilini—showcasing the very best that the island has to offer. If you have trouble sourcing razor clams, this dish is also beautiful with other types of clams or mussels.

To clean the razor clams, place in a large bowl and cover with cold water. Leave for a couple of hours, drain and then repeat the process.

To cook the clams, heat the oil and garlic in a large frying pan over medium heat for 1 minute, stirring continuously to ensure the garlic does not brown. Add the razor clams and stir through.

Add the white wine, and then the cherry tomatoes, crushing them with your hands as you place them in the pan. Cover with a lid, turn the heat to high, and cook for 2–3 minutes, until the clams have opened.

Add the parsley, season with salt and pepper, and stir gently.

Serve the clams in a bowl with their cooking juices. Drizzle with extra virgin olive oil to taste.

—Serves 4

GRILLED OCTOPUS AND BLACK-EYED PEA SALAD
with MESSOLONGHI BOTTARGA

Prep Time 15 minutes, plus overnight soaking of peas
Cooking Time 1 hour 40 minutes

Black-eyed pea salad
1½ cups (10½ oz/280 g) dried
    black-eyed peas
1 bay leaf
1½ tomatoes, diced
½ red onion, finely diced
1 garlic clove, sliced
3 tablespoons chopped oregano
¾ cup (185 ml) extra virgin
    olive oil, plus extra for drizzling
3 tablespoons lemon juice
Sea salt and freshly ground
    black pepper

Grilled octopus
2 lb 4 oz (1 kg) octopus
    tentacles (large)
½ cup (125 ml) extra virgin
    olive oil

⅛ oz (5 g) Messolonghi
    bottarga, finely grated

Black-eyed peas and octopus are classic ingredients of the Greek islands, found in one version or another on almost every taverna menu. Here I've added a special element: Messolonghi bottarga, known as the Greek caviar. This is grated over the top just before serving to add a beautiful, textural burst of freshness, color, and flavor.

To make the black-eyed pea salad, place the peas and bay leaf in a pan and cover with water to cover the peas by 1¼ inches (3 cm). Bring to a boil, then allow to cool and leave to soak in the refrigerator for 24 hours.

Drain the peas, discarding the bay leaf, and rinse. Return to a clean pan and cover with water. Bring to a boil, then simmer for 40–50 minutes until tender. Drain, then cool.

Meanwhile, to make the grilled octopus, place the octopus in a large pan of boiling salted water, reduce the heat, and simmer for 90 minutes until tender. Leave to cool in the cooking liquid.

Mix the cooled peas with the tomato, red onion, garlic, oregano, olive oil, and lemon juice and season with salt and pepper. Toss together.

Remove the cooled octopus from the water, toss with the olive oil, and season with salt and pepper. Preheat a grill or grill pan until hot and cook the octopus for 2–3 minutes on each side.

Serve the octopus with the black-eyed pea salad. Finish with finely grated bottarga over the top and a drizzle of extra virgin olive oil.

—Serves 6

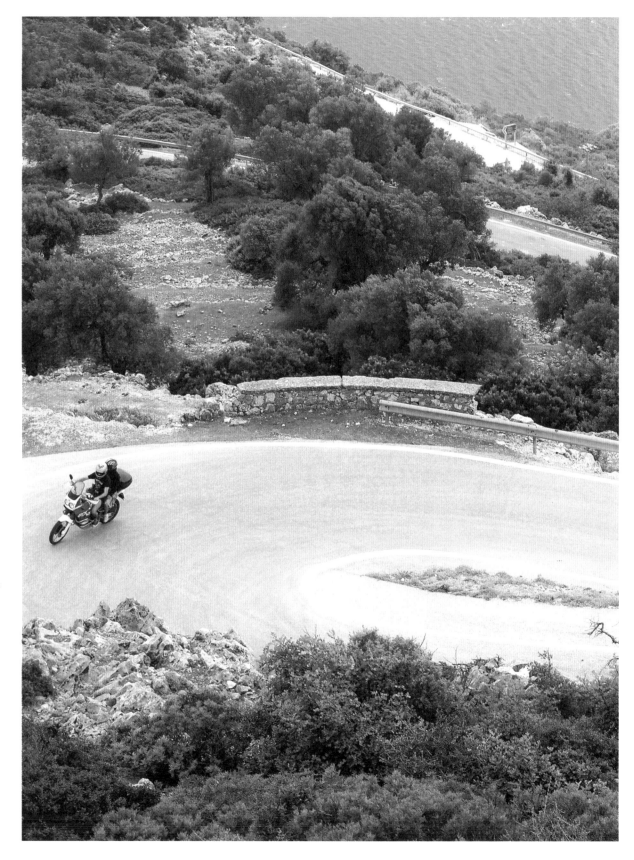

LEFKADA SALAMI AND GRAVIERA CHEESE *with* PICKLES

Prep Time 25 minutes, plus 48 hours pickling
Cooking Time 5 minutes

14 oz (400 g) Lefkada salami,
finely sliced (or any quality
cured pork sausage with
a high black pepper content)
8½ oz (245 g) Graviera cheese,
sliced into triangular wedges
8 slices crusty bread

**Pickled baby bell peppers
and long chilies**
10½ oz (300 g) baby bell peppers
10½ oz (300 g) long chilies
2½ cups (625 ml) white
wine vinegar
3 tablespoons sugar
3 tablespoons salt
2 bay leaves
1 tablespoon fennel seeds
3 garlic cloves, sliced
2 tablespoons black peppercorns

**Tomato, red onion, pepper,
and wild caper salad**
5½ oz (150 g) cherry tomatoes,
cut in half
¼ red onion, finely diced
¼ cup (1½ oz/40 g) finely diced
red pepper
¼ cup (1½ oz/40 g) finely diced
yellow pepper
¼ cup (1½ oz/40 g) finely diced
green pepper
1 tablespoon wild capers
½ cup (125 ml) extra virgin
olive oil
Sea salt and freshly ground
black pepper

As mentioned in the chapter introduction, the Greek island of Lefkada was settled by people from the Venetian island of Burano. Despite being most well known for fishing, the people of Burano brought with them and shared their expertise in charcuterie making. Today Lefkada is renowned throughout the whole of Greece for its amazing, high-quality spicy salami, made with garlic and peppercorns.

To make the pickled baby bell peppers and long chilies, remove the cores from the baby bell peppers and shake out any seeds. Pack the cored baby bell peppers and whole long chilies into separate sterilized pickling jars.

Put the vinegar, sugar, salt, bay leaves, fennel seeds, garlic, and peppercorns in a pan with 2½ cups (625 ml) water. Bring to a boil.

Pour the hot pickling liquid over both the peppers and chilies in the jars, making sure they are completely covered. When cool, seal the jars and refrigerate for at least 48 hours.

To make the salad, combine the tomatoes, onion, peppers, and wild capers in a bowl and dress with the olive oil. Season with salt and pepper and toss together.

Serve the salami and cheese on a platter with 8 pickled bell peppers, 4 long chilies, a bowl of tomato and red onion salad, and the crusty bread.

—Serves 8

Pasta, rice, and pies

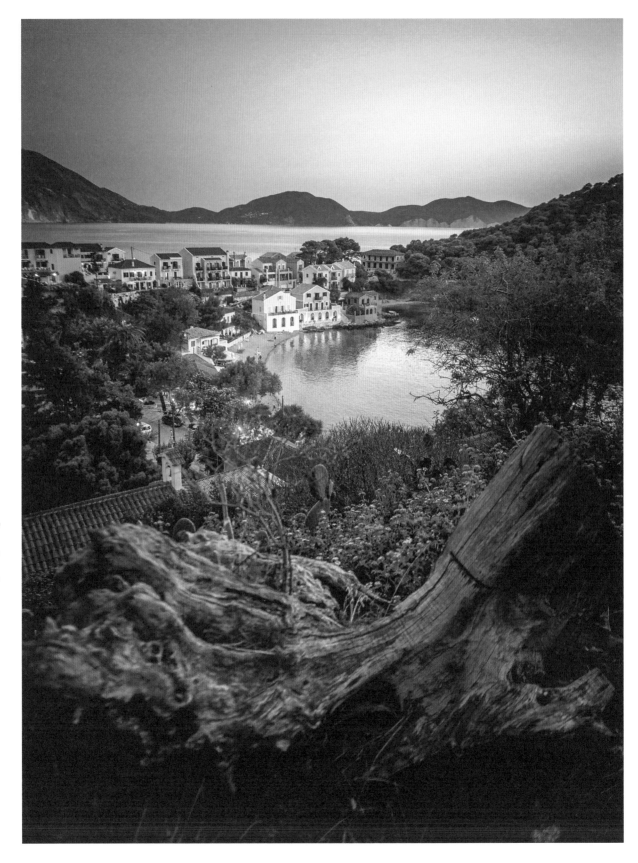

CEPHALONIAN SALT COD PIE

Prep Time 30 minutes, plus 48 hours soaking the salt cod and 40 minutes resting the dough
Cooking Time 1 hour 15 minutes

1 lb 5 oz (600 g) salt cod (*baccala*)
¾ cup (175 ml) extra virgin olive
    oil, plus extra for greasing
3 onions, finely sliced
6 garlic cloves, chopped
2 tomatoes, peeled and chopped
1 cup (9 oz/250 g) tomato
    paste
½ cup (3½ oz/100 g) rice
3 tablespoons chopped oregano
3 tablespoons chopped parsley
2 cups (3½ oz/100 g) spinach,
    chopped
½ teaspoon allspice
Sea salt and freshly ground
    black pepper

Shortcrust pastry crust
3⅓ cups (1 lb 2oz/500 g) all-
    purpose flour, plus extra for
    dusting
3⅓ sticks (13½ oz/380 g) butter,
    chilled and diced
A large pinch salt
2 egg yolks
¼ cup (60 ml) chilled water
1 egg, lightly beaten, for egg wash

Another example of the strong Venetian influence on the cuisine of the Greek islands, the star of this recipe is, of course, the salt cod—a real legacy of the Venetian Republic and an ingredient that has been embraced in many different forms throughout the Mediterranean. Also key to this dish are the onions, which imbue a lovely sweetness that balances the saltiness of the fish.

Wash the excess salt from the cod, then soak in cold water in the fridge for 48 hours, changing the water twice daily. This process will remove most of the fish's saltiness.

In a saucepan, bring 3¼ cups (800 ml) water to a boil and poach the cod for 5–10 minutes, making sure it is covered with the water. Drain, keeping the poaching liquid. Remove all the bones from the cod and finely chop the flesh. Set aside.

To make the shortcrust pastry, place the flour, butter, and salt in a food processor and mix to fine crumbs. Add the egg yolks and water and process until a dough ball starts to form, taking care not to overwork the dough.

Place the dough on a lightly floured tray, cover with plastic wrap, and leave to rest in the fridge for 40 minutes.

Preheat the oven to 350°F (180°C).

In a large pan, heat the olive oil over medium heat for 1 minute. Add the onion and cook until translucent. Add the garlic and cook for 2 minutes.

Add the cod, tomatoes, and tomato paste to the pan and stir through. Add the rice and 2 cups (500 ml) of the poaching liquid. Bring to a boil and cook for another 10 minutes. Add the oregano, parsley, spinach, and allspice. Cook for a further 5 minutes, then season with salt and pepper and leave to cool.

Remove the pastry from the fridge and place on a lightly floured work surface. Divide the dough in half. Using a rolling pin, roll into two ½ inch (1 cm) thick, 7 × 5 inch (18 × 13 cm) rectangles.

Lightly grease an 7 × 5 inch (18 × 13 cm) baking dish with olive oil. Line the dish with one piece of pastry. Pour the filling into the dish and cover with the remaining pastry rectangle. Crimp the pastry together around the edge, removing any excess. Make two small holes in the top to allow steam to escape during cooking.

Lightly whisk the egg with a dash of water and brush over the pie. Bake in the oven for 45 minutes or until the pastry is golden. Cool for 15 minutes before cutting.

—*Serves 6*

GOGGES PASTA *with* BROWN BUTTER *and* MYZITHRA SALTED RICOTTA

Prep Time 30 minutes, plus resting the dough
Cooking Time 25 minutes

Sauce
½ cup (2 oz/60 g) walnuts, chopped
1 tablespoon (½ oz/15 g) butter
3 tablespoons olive oil
3 tablespoons dried Myzithra or salted goat milk ricotta, grated, plus extra to garnish
Sea salt

Gogges pasta
3 cups (1 lb 2 oz/500 g) fine semolina
1 teaspoon salt
2 tablespoons olive oil

With brown butter and salted ricotta, this dish looks and feels like it could easily belong in Italy. Having said that, two key elements are classically Greek. The first is the gogges pasta, which hails from the Peloponnese and is worth the effort to make, and the second is Myzithra—a traditional unpasteurized Greek ricotta cheese that's available both fresh (creamy and spreadable in consistency) and dried (salty and most commonly used grated over pasta, as in this dish).

Preheat the oven to 325°F (170°C). Arrange the walnuts evenly on a baking sheet and roast for 3–5 minutes, or until golden brown. Remove from the oven and transfer to a plate to prevent over-coloring. Allow to cool completely before coarsely chopping.

To make the pasta, mix together the semolina and salt in a bowl. Gradually add 1 cup (250 ml) water and knead to a smooth dough.

Add the olive oil and knead again to combine. Cover with plastic wrap and leave to rest for 30 minutes.

Divide the dough into 5½ oz (150 g) pieces; roll each piece into a log about ½ inch (1 cm) wide and cut into ¾ inch (2 cm) lengths.

Take a piece of dough and, using your thumb, press onto a floured wooden ridged pasta board and roll down to form a sea shell shape. If you don't have a ridged board, use a floured work surface: the pasta will be smooth but will still work. Continue until all the dough is used. Store on a floured tray, making sure the pasta shapes are not touching, until ready to cook.

Bring a large pan of salted water to a boil and cook the pasta for 12–15 minutes: the pasta is intended to be quite firm, but if you prefer a softer texture, cook for a little longer. Drain the pasta and place in a serving bowl.

In a frying pan, heat the butter and olive oil over medium heat until the butter begins to foam. Add the cheese and cook until golden brown. Pour the sauce over the pasta and sprinkle with the walnuts. Season and serve with extra cheese over the top.

—Serves 4

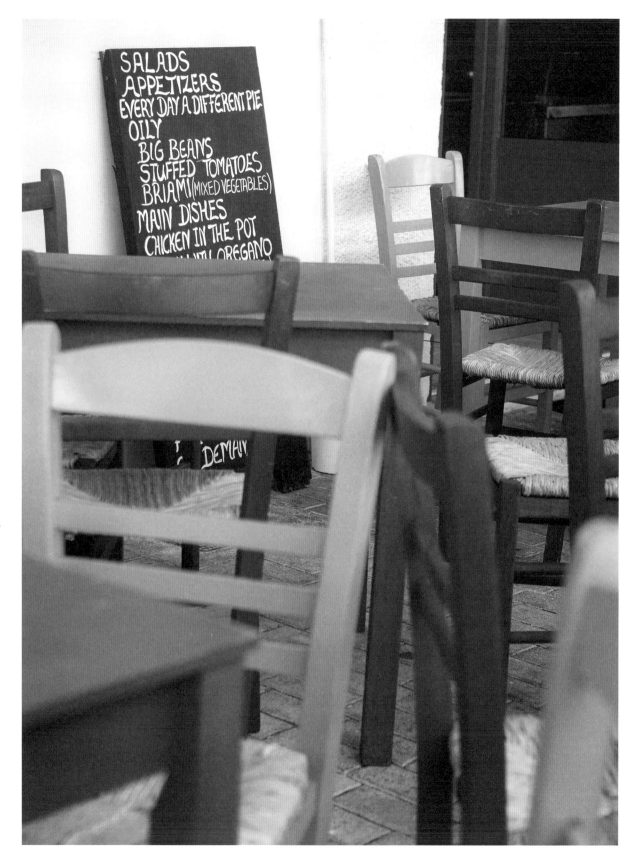

CORFIOT PASTITSADA *with* BUCATINI

Prep Time 10 minutes
Cooking Time 1 hour 30 minutes

½ cup (125 ml) extra virgin olive oil
4 chicken leg quarters
1 onion, finely diced
4 garlic cloves, crushed
1 cinnamon stick
¼ teaspoon ground nutmeg
1 bay leaf
Scant ½ cup (100 ml) red
  wine vinegar
8 tomatoes, cored and chopped
1 tablespoon tomato paste
2 cups (500 ml) Chicken Stock
  (page 236)
10½ oz (300 g) dried bucatini
  pasta
Grated Kefalotyri, Kefalograviera,
  or Graviera cheese, to taste
Sea salt and freshly ground
  black pepper

Yet another interpretation of *pastissada*—many iterations of which are scattered throughout the Mediterranean. This one is traditionally made with cockerel, or young rooster, and is typical of what you see on almost every Greek island. Here, I'm using the whole chicken hindquarter and serving it with pasta, something not seen with *pastissada* dishes along the Croatian coast or in Italy.

Heat the olive oil in a saucepan over high heat for 1 minute. Add the chicken, skin-side down, and cook until the skin is golden brown. Turn the chicken pieces and cook for another minute. Remove from the pan and set aside.

Turn the heat to low, add the onion and garlic, and cook until the onion is translucent. Add the spices and bay leaf and cook gently for 3–4 minutes, stirring regularly.

Return the chicken to the pan and pour in the vinegar to deglaze the bottom of the pan. Stir in the tomatoes, tomato paste, and stock. Season with sea salt and pepper. Cook for 40–60 minutes until the chicken is tender and starting to fall off the bone. Adjust the seasoning if needed.

Cook the bucatini in a deep pot of boiling salted water until al dente.

Remove the chicken from the sauce and fold the pasta through the sauce. Serve the chicken on top of the bucatini. Sprinkle with grated Kefalotyri, Kefalograviera, or Graviera cheese, to taste.

—*Serves 4*

SEAFOOD ASSYRTIKO GIOUVETSI

Prep Time 20 minutes
Cooking Time 30 minutes

½ cup (125 ml) extra virgin olive oil, plus extra for drizzling
2 cups (11 oz/310 g) finely diced onion
1 cup (2 oz/60 g) finely diced fennel
1 cup (2 oz/60 g) mild red chilies, diced
1 tablespoon sweet paprika
4 garlic cloves, crushed
1½ cups (9 oz/250 g) orzo pasta
1½ cups (375 ml) Assyrtiko white wine (or any aromatic white wine)
4 cups (1 liter) Crustacean Broth (page 239)
1 tablespoon tomato paste
7 oz (200 g) clams
7 oz (200 g) black mussels
7 oz (200 g) calamari, cleaned and cut into ½ inch (1 cm) thick slices
7 oz (200 g) scorpion fish fillet (or any white fish)
7 oz (200 g) shrimp, peeled, deveined, and cut into ¾ inch (2 cm) pieces
½ cup (1 oz/30 g) chopped parsley
Sea salt and freshly ground black pepper

With such an abundance of quality fresh seafood, this dish is a staple on the island of Santorini. Giouvetsi is common throughout much of Greece, often with meat instead of seafood, but fish is more commonly used on many of the islands. The juggernaut indigenous Santorini white wine used in this recipe, Assyrtiko, is also a feature, and is a stunning wine to enjoy with the dish.

Heat the olive oil in a saucepan over low heat. Add the onion, fennel, chilies, paprika, and garlic and cook for 3–4 minutes or until the onion is translucent. Season with salt and pepper.

Add the orzo pasta to the pan and stir through. Add the wine and stir to deglaze the pan, then cook for 4 minutes to cook off the alcohol. Add the crustacean broth and tomato paste and simmer over medium heat for 12 minutes.

Add the clams and mussels to the pan and cook for 2 minutes, then add the calamari, scorpion fish, and shrimp and cook for 3 minutes or until just cooked.

Add salt and pepper if needed and stir in the parsley. Drizzle with a little extra virgin olive oil to serve.

—*Serves 4*

IONIAN WILD WEED AND NATIVE ASPARAGUS MACARONI CHEESE

Prep Time 15 minutes
Cooking Time 1 hour 30 minutes

4½ oz (125 g) dried pennette pasta
Generous ½ cup (150 ml) extra virgin olive oil
7 oz (200 g) wild greens—any combination of Greek *horta* greens, Greek *vlita* (amaranth), spinach, beet greens, kale, any chard, or silver beet, roughly chopped
7 oz (200 g) native asparagus, roughly chopped (or regular green asparagus)
1 large leek, chopped
2 garlic cloves, finely chopped
8 oz (225 g) Greek feta cheese, crumbled
8 oz (225 g) Graviera or Kefalograviera cheese, finely grated
1 cup (8 oz/225 g) fresh ricotta cheese
Pinch of nutmeg
4 filo pastry sheets
3 tablespoons (1½ oz/40 g) butter, melted
2 tablespoons (¾ oz/20 g) sesame seeds
Sea salt and freshly ground black pepper

Pastitsio is a classic baked pasta dish in Greece, usually comprising pennette or macaroni, ground meat, and béchamel sauce. This is a fantastic vegetarian version, which also draws on key elements from another Greek favorite— wild weed pie. I've omitted *pastitsio's* béchamel and replaced the meat with a range of bright and wonderful wild greens, including the indigenous *horta*, *vlita*, and native asparagus. Feel free to use as many greens as you like, with chard, spinach, and green asparagus making great substitutes.

Preheat the oven to 350°F (180°C).

Bring a large pot of salted water to a boil and cook the pennette pasta until just tender. Drain, toss in 3 tablespoons of the olive oil, and set aside.

Wash the wild greens and asparagus in cold water.

In a large frying pan, heat the remaining olive oil over low heat, add the leek and garlic, and cook for 5–10 minutes until the leek has completely softened. Add the wild weeds and asparagus and cook until the leafy greens have wilted and the asparagus softened. Season with sea salt and pepper and cook, stirring constantly, over low heat for another 5 minutes. (Be careful with the seasoning as the cheeses added later will add salt.)

Transfer the mixture to a bowl and add the feta, Graviera or Kefalograviera cheese, ricotta, and nutmeg and stir well. Mix in the cooked pennette. Adjust the seasoning if needed and spoon into a lightly greased 9½ x 12½ inch (24 × 32 cm) baking dish.

Brush each sheet of filo on both sides with melted butter. Lay the filo sheets on top of the wild weed and asparagus mixture and sprinkle with sesame seeds.

Bake for 55 minutes, or until golden.

—Serves 6

SPICY LOBSTER LINGUINI

Prep Time 25 minutes
Cooking Time 1 hour

1 × 2 lb 4 oz–2 lb 10 oz (1–1.2 kg) live lobster
Generous ½ cup (150 ml) extra virgin olive oil
1 white onion, finely diced
4 garlic cloves, chopped
½ cup (125 ml) Metaxa brandy (or any quality brandy)
1 cup (250 ml) white wine
6 ripe tomatoes, diced
2 cups (500 ml) Crustacean Broth (page 239)
½ teaspoon dried red pepper flakes
½ cup (¾ oz/20 g) basil leaves, chopped
2 tablespoons chopped parsley
1 lb 5 oz (600 g) dried linguini
1 tablespoon (½ oz/15 g) butter
Sea salt and freshly ground black pepper

This is a special occasion dish, usually served in high-end restaurants and showcasing some of the best flavors of Mediterranean Greece, including fresh lobster and Metaxa, an iconic Greek brandy. I've taken the liberty of adding a pinch of dried chili—something not commonly found in Greek cuisine—adding a lovely heat to the dish.

Place the lobster in the freezer for 10 minutes before cooking.

Fill a large pot with salted water and bring to a boil over high heat. Place the lobster in the water and cook for approximately 5–7 minutes, depending on the size. Remove the lobster and place into iced water to stop the cooking process.

When the lobster is chilled, cut in half and carefully remove the meat from the tail. The meat will be largely raw except for the flesh near the shell. Dice into 1 inch (2.5 cm) pieces, reserve the head for serving.

To make the sauce, heat the olive oil in a saucepan over low heat, add the onion, and cook until translucent. Add the garlic and cook for 1 minute. Add the brandy and cook for 2 minutes. Add the white wine and cook for 2 minutes. Add the tomatoes, broth, red pepper flakes, basil, and parsley and simmer over medium heat for 25–30 minutes.

Before serving, heat the lobster head in a hot oven, in boiling water, or under a broiler for 10 minutes.

Meanwhile, cook the pasta in a large pot of boiling salted water for 9–13 minutes or until al dente. Just before the pasta is ready, add the lobster meat and butter to the sauce, giving the lobster 3 minutes to cook through before serving. Season with salt and pepper.

Drain the pasta and toss through the sauce. Serve on a platter and decorate with the warm lobster head.

—Serves 4

Mains

CYPRIAN SLOW-COOKED CALAMARI STIFADO

Prep Time 10 minutes
Cooking Time 1 hour 10 minutes

1 cup (250 ml) extra virgin olive oil, plus extra for drizzling
1 onion, finely diced
4 garlic cloves, crushed
1 cup (250 ml) Xynisteri white wine (or any quality dry white wine)
6 cups (3 lb 8 oz/1.6 kg) chopped tomatoes
2 tablespoons tomato paste
2 bay leaves
½ tablespoon Greek oregano
2 lb 4 oz (1 kg) small whole calamari, cleaned
8 baby potatoes, cut in half
2 tablespoons chopped parsley (optional)
Sea salt and freshly ground black pepper

The method of slow cooking in Greece is known as *stifado*; in Italy it's *stufato*, based on the Italian word for stove—*stufa*. While commonly reserved for meats, slow cooking can be used for calamari and octopus too, delivering stunning results. The base ingredients of white wine, olive oil, bay leaf, onion, garlic, and tomato create great flavor in this dish. For a more intense version, the white wine can be substituted for any quality medium-bodied red wine—my wife's favorite!

Place the olive oil and onion in a large saucepan over low heat and cook until the onion is translucent.

Add the garlic and cook for 1 minute. Add the white wine and cook for 2 minutes. Add the tomatoes, tomato paste, bay leaves, oregano, and 2 cups (500 ml) water and bring to a simmer.

Add the calamari and potatoes and cook over low heat for 30–60 minutes, or until tender. Season with salt and pepper and, if you like, garnish with chopped parsley. Finish with a drizzle of extra virgin olive oil.

—Serves 4

ITHACAN SLOW-ROASTED ISLAND GOAT *with* FRESH OREGANO

Prep Time 15 minutes
Cooking Time 5 hours 10 minutes

8 garlic cloves, 2 finely chopped, 6 left whole
1 cup (¾ oz/20 g) fresh island oregano (or any fresh oregano)
3 lb 2 oz (1.4 kg) kid goat shoulder, bone in
1 cup (250 ml) lemon juice
1 cup (250 ml) extra virgin olive oil, plus extra for drizzling
2 cups (500 ml) Chicken Stock (page 236)
2 lb 4 oz (1 kg) potatoes, peeled and cutt into ¾ inch (2 cm) thick slices
Sea salt and freshly ground black pepper

Goat from Ithaca, the island where my wife Krissoula's family still lives, would have to be some of the very best meat I've ever eaten. Krissoula's cousins are shepherds, and their herd of goats eat any number of the roughly 33 different wild herbs on the island, including thyme and sage, which imparts a very distinctive and unique flavor into their meat. Every time we visit we feast on a goat, spit roasted until the meat is literally falling off the bone. It's absolute heaven, and always a highlight of our trip. If you're not lucky enough to have a spit roast at your disposal, oven roasting will create a stunning result too.

Preheat the oven to 400°F (200°C).

Form a bed in a roasting pan with half the oregano and the whole garlic cloves.

Smother the goat shoulder with the chopped garlic and season with salt and black pepper. Place the goat shoulder on top of the herbs and garlic in the pan. Drizzle with lemon juice and half of the olive oil.

Cover the pan with foil and roast for 30 minutes. Reduce the oven to 300°F (150°C) and add the stock to the pan. Continue to cook, covered, for a further 3½–4 hours, turning halfway through, until the goat is very tender. Remove the foil and increase the oven temperature to 350°F (180°C) for the last 20 minutes to color the meat.

Remove the goat from the pan, cover with foil, and keep warm.

Place the potatoes in the same roasting pan and drizzle with the remaining oil. Season with salt and pepper and return to the oven at 350°F (180°C). Roast for 40 minutes, turning halfway through the cooking.

Serve the goat with the roasted potatoes and pan juices, garnished with the remaining chopped oregano and extra olive oil, if you like.

—*Serves 8*

SWEET-AND-SOUR RED MULLET FROM CRETE

Prep Time 5 minutes
Cooking Time 25 minutes

4 large red mullets, scaled
    and gutted
½ tablespoon sea salt
All-purpose flour, for coating fish
½ cup (125 ml) extra virgin olive oil
4 garlic cloves, sliced
2 sprigs rosemary
½ cup (125 ml) white wine vinegar
Scant 1 cup (5½ oz/150 g) black
    raisins

This is a dish you'll find throughout most of the formerly Venetian-ruled Greek islands, not to mention the Republic's other key Mediterranean territories. The original Venetian dish *in saor*, which means "to add flavor" (called *savoro* in Greece), was really borne out of necessity, with fishermen using vinegar in an attempt to preserve the abundance of freshly caught fish. In Italy and Greece less vinegar is used today than in the past and, unlike the Venetian version, Greeks do not often incorporate onions, but add their own unique touch with rosemary and garlic instead.

Preheat the oven to 350°F (180°C).

Season the fish with sea salt, then coat with a dusting of flour.

Heat half the olive oil in a large frying pan for 1 minute. Add the fish and cook on each side for 2 minutes.

Transfer the fish to a baking sheet and roast until just cooked—the timing will depend on the size of the fish: a medium fish will take 5 minutes to cook, a larger fish will take 10 minutes. The meat at the back of the head should just be coming away from the bone.

Meanwhile, in a small pan, heat the remaining olive oil, garlic, and rosemary over low heat for 1 minute. Add the vinegar and raisins and then simmer for 10 minutes.

Place the fish on a serving dish and pour the vinegar dressing over the top. Let it cool and serve the fish at room temperature.

—Serves 4

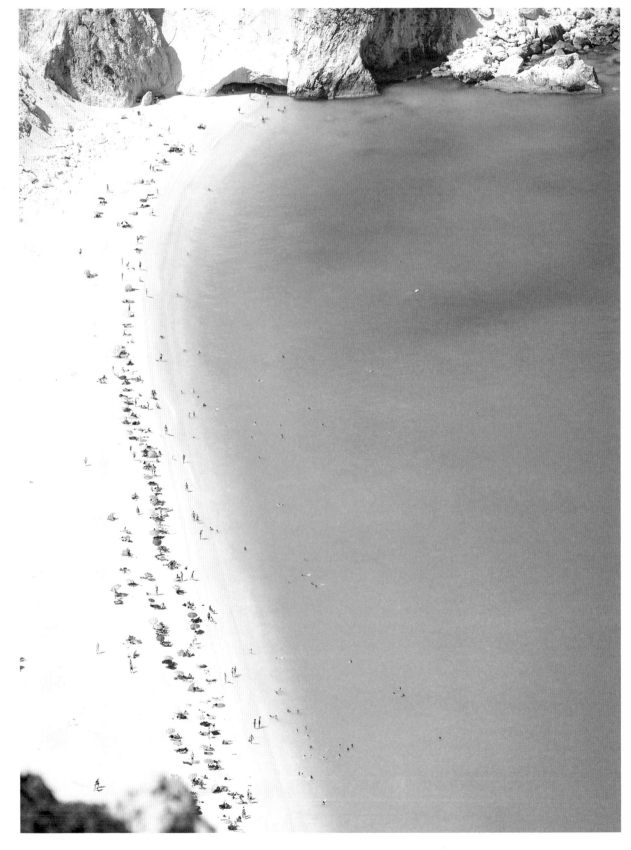

CORFU-STYLE JOHN DORY
COOKED IN WHITE WINE *with* WILD GREENS

Prep Time 10 minutes
Cooking Time 50 minutes

1¼ cups (300 ml) extra virgin olive oil, plus extra to mix with lemon juice
½ white onion, thinly sliced
8 garlic cloves, chopped
1 cup (250 ml) Corfiot Kakotrygis white wine (or any quality dry white wine)
½ cup (125 ml) lemon juice
1 lb 2 oz (500 g) potatoes, peeled and sliced into ¾ inch (2 cm) thick pieces
2 cups (500 ml) Fish Stock (page 236)
1 tablespoon oregano leaves
1 tablespoon rosemary leaves
1 lb 5 oz (600 g) John Dory fillets
Sea salt and freshly ground black pepper

Wild greens
2 lb (900 g) Greek *vlita* (amaranth)
3 tablespoons extra virgin olive oil
Juice of 1 lemon
2 teaspoons sea salt

This is a classic example of *"in bianco,"* a term used in Italian cooking to denote a "white" dish—that is, where tomatoes or red wine aren't used. It usually suggests the inclusion of white wine and has, over generations, been wholeheartedly embraced in Corfu, by far the most Venetian influenced of all the Greek islands. This recipe uses fillets, but it's also fantastic with a whole fish—you'll just need to adjust the cooking time accordingly.

Heat half the olive oil in a large frying pan over low heat. Add the onion and half the garlic and cook until soft and translucent. Add the wine and half the lemon juice and cook until the wine has almost evaporated.

Stir in the potatoes and cook for 2 minutes. Add the fish stock, half the oregano, and half the rosemary and season with salt and pepper. Turn the heat to medium and cook for 15 minutes or until the potatoes are cooked through.

Meanwhile, for the wild greens, trim the thick stems from the base of the amaranth and rinse well. Bring a large pot of salted water to a boil. Add the greens and cook for 10–15 minutes until tender. Drain and dress with the olive oil, lemon juice, and salt. Serve warm or at room temperature.

Place the John Dory on top of the potatoes in the pan. Add the remaining garlic and drizzle with the remaining oil. Cook for about 5 minutes, until the fish is just cooked through.

Mix the remaining lemon juice with a little extra virgin olive oil and toss with the remaining oregano and rosemary.

Serve the John Dory with the potatoes and pan juices on a platter. Garnish with the fresh herbs and lemon juice mixture and serve alongside the wild greens.

—Serves 4

RABBIT STIFADO *with* GRAVIERA CHEESE *and* POLENTA BREAD

Prep Time 40 minutes, plus 2–3 hours marinating
Cooking Time 3 hours 20 minutes

1 × 2 lb 4 oz–3 lb 5 oz (1–1.5 kg) rabbit, cut into 8 pieces
Generous ½ cup (150 ml) white wine vinegar
10½ tablespoons (5½ oz/160 g) butter
1 cup (5½ oz/160 g) diced onion
4 garlic cloves, finely diced
1 cup (5½ oz/160 g) diced carrot
1 cup (5 oz/140 g) diced celery
1 cup (4½ oz/130 g) diced leek
2 cups (500 ml) red wine
3 bay leaves
2 cloves
1 cinnamon stick
3 tablespoons tomato paste
6 cups (1.5 liters) Chicken Stock (page 236)
9 oz (250 g) Graviera cheese, broken into ¾ inch (2 cm) pieces
Sea salt and freshly ground black pepper

Polenta bread
1 cup (5½ oz/150 g) all-purpose flour
2 cups (13½ oz/380 g) fine grain polenta cornmeal
2½ teaspoons baking powder
1 teaspoon salt
1½ tablespoons honey
3 eggs
2½ cups (600 ml) Buttermilk (page 243)
2½ sticks (10½ oz/300 g) butter, melted
6½ oz (180 g) quality feta, crumbled

Rabbit is a very popular ingredient for Greek *stifado*, which is made in many regions. In this recipe the rabbit is served with polenta bread, traditionally eaten in Greece as a dessert. I've tweaked it to create a more modern, savory version, which is fantastic with most braised dishes.

Place the rabbit in a large bowl, cover with the vinegar and marinate for 2–3 hours. Drain and pat dry with paper towels.

Heat a large Dutch oven over medium heat. Add the butter and rabbit pieces and cook gently for 5 minutes, turning as the rabbit browns. Lightly season with salt and pepper (not too much salt as the Graviera cheese is salty).

Remove the rabbit from the pot. Add the onion, garlic, carrot, celery, and leek to the pot and cook until starting to brown. Return the rabbit to the pot and then add the wine, bay leaves, cloves, cinnamon, and tomato paste and cook for about 10 minutes until the wine has almost evaporated.

Add the stock and cook over low heat for 3 hours or until the meat is falling off the bone.

Add the Graviera cheese and cook for 10 minutes until the cheese is soft but not completely melted.

Meanwhile, preheat the oven to 350°F (180°C).

For the polenta bread, mix together the flour, polenta, baking powder, and salt in a large mixing bowl.

Whisk together the honey, eggs, buttermilk, and 4 tablespoons of the melted butter in a bowl.

Heat a 10 × 5 × 2 inch (24 × 12 × 6 cm) baking dish in the oven. When hot, coat the inside of the baking dish thoroughly with the remaining butter (I use paper towels to get into all corners of the dish).

Combine the honey mixture with the polenta mixture and 3½ oz (100 g) of the feta cheese, then pour into the baking dish, spreading evenly. Sprinkle the remaining feta over the top and bake for 25–35 minutes, until cooked through.

Arrange the rabbit on a serving platter and serve with the cooking juices and polenta bread.

Note
Leftover polenta bread is great toasted and served with fresh butter.

—Serves 6

ROASTED PORK LOIN *with* BRAISED ARTICHOKES *and* BABY FAVA BEANS

Prep Time 20 minutes, plus overnight refrigeration of pork
Cooking Time 1 hour 30 minutes

6 lb 12 oz (3 kg) rolled pork loin
(ask a butcher to roll and tie a
pork loin with the belly
attached in 1¼–1½ inch/3–4 cm
intervals and score the skin
between the ties)
3 tablespoons sea salt
Scant ½ cup (100 ml) extra
virgin olive oil

**Braised artichokes
and baby fava beans**
1 lemon, cut in half
3 globe artichokes
1 lb 2 oz (500 g) baby fava beans
1½ cups (350 ml) extra
virgin olive oil, plus extra
for drizzling
2 onions, roughly chopped
4 garlic cloves, finely chopped
3 ripe tomatoes, cored
and roughly chopped
Sea salt and freshly ground
black pepper

I'm sorry to say that not many people cook for me these days. Many other chefs will tell you they have the same problem. Thankfully, my mother-in-law, Maria, is an exception, and a wonderful one at that. This is probably my favorite dish of hers, although she has many greats. I particularly love the braised artichokes and fava beans—a simple but fantastic combination—and if it wasn't for Maria, I wouldn't know the joy of cooking and eating fava beans whole. To cook them this way, choose small, early-harvest fava beans as they will be the most tender.

Preheat the oven to 500°F (250°C).

For the roasted pork loin, bring 20 cups (5 liters) water to the boil. Place the pork on a cooling rack over a sink and carefully pour the boiling water over the pork skin, turning to ensure it is all rendered. Rub the sea salt into the skin and refrigerate, uncovered, overnight.

Remove from the refrigerator and bring the pork to room temperature. Add the olive oil to a roasting pan and heat in the oven for 8 minutes. Remove from the oven and place the pork in the pan, turning as the skin blisters all over. Reduce the oven to 400°F (200°C) and roast the pork for 90 minutes, turning every 10–15 minutes. Let the pork rest for 30–40 minutes before carving.

Meanwhile, for the braised artichokes and fava beans, squeeze half the lemon into a bowl of cold water. Remove the outer leaves of the artichokes, then, using a spoon, scoop out the center choke and peel the stem using a vegetable peeler. Rub the artichokes all over with the other lemon half as you do this to prevent them discoloring. Cut the artichokes into quarters and store in the cold lemon water.

Trim the ends off the young fava beans (do not shell or peel). Leave whole if they are small but cut in half, on an angle, if they are large. You want them to be no longer than a large green bean.

Place the extra virgin olive oil and onion in a large saucepan over low heat and cook until translucent. Add the garlic and cook for 1 minute. Stir in the tomato.

Drain the artichokes and add to the pan. Add the fava beans and season with salt and pepper. Add enough water to almost cover the ingredients—don't add too much water, or you'll dilute the flavor of the dish and its liquid.

Bring to a simmer and gently cook the artichokes and beans for 25 minutes or until completely tender, stirring gently throughout.

Slice the pork into 1 inch (2.5 cm) thick slices. Serve with the braised artichokes and fava beans and season with olive oil and freshly ground black pepper.

—Serves 6

Dolci

CORFU MAVRODAPHNE ZABAGLIONE
with ROSEWATER WALNUT COOKIES

Prep Time 15 minutes
Cooking Time 25 minutes

Walnut cookies
1½ cups (6½ oz/185 g)
    confectioners' sugar, plus
    3 tablespoons for the cookies
9 tablespoons (4½ oz/125 g)
    butter, softened
½ teaspoon rosewater
1 cup (4½ oz/125 g) all-purpose
    flour
¾ cup (3 oz/90 g) walnuts,
    chopped

Zabaglione
8 egg yolks
½ cup (3½ oz/110 g) sugar
½ cup (125 ml) Mavrodaphne
    wine (or any quality fortified
    sweet red wine)

Zabaglione, a light dessert made with egg yolks, sugar, and Marsala, is famous in Italy—and in Corfu too. It is yet another linguistic and culinary marriage between the two countries. Being the most Italian of the Greek islands, I wasn't surprised to spot this dish in Corfu: as far as I've seen it's the only one of the Greek islands to offer it as part of its dessert repertoire. They do a great job of it, too, using Greece's indigenous fortified sweet wine variety, Mavrodaphne, in place of Marsala.

To make the walnut cookies, preheat the oven to 350°F (180°C) and spread the confectioners' sugar evenly on a tray.

In a mixing bowl, whisk together the butter and rosewater. Sift together the flour and 3 tablespoons confectioners' sugar, then beat into the butter. Fold in the walnuts.

Roll the dough into 1 inch (2.5 cm) balls and arrange on a baking sheet spaced 2 inches (5 cm) apart. Bake in the oven for 12 minutes. Immediately roll the cookies in the confectoners' sugar on the tray and set aside to cool.

To make the zabaglione, half-fill a pot with water and bring to a simmer over medium heat. In a large heat-resistant bowl, whisk the egg yolks, sugar, and wine together. Place the bowl over the pot of simmering water and whisk for 10 minutes, until the mixture thickens to the consistency of light custard.

Pour the zabaglione into serving glasses. When the cookies are cool, roll once again in the confectioners' sugar and serve with the zabaglione.

—Serves 4

IONIAN PLUM TART

Prep Time 30 minutes, plus 30 minutes to rest the dough
Cooking Time 45 minutes

13 tablespoons (6½ oz/180 g) butter, softened, plus extra for greasing
1⅓ cups (6 oz/165 g) confectioners' sugar
2 eggs
½ tablespoon vanilla extract
2 cups (9 oz/260 g) 00 flour, sifted
1 pinch of salt
1⅓ cups (4½ oz/125 g) ground almonds

Plum jam
1 lb 2 oz (500 g) plums, pitted and quartered
1 tablespoon lemon juice
3 cups (1 lb 6 oz/625 g) sugar

Whipped cream
1 cup (250 ml) heavy whipping cream
1 tablespoon confectioners' sugar, sifted
Seeds from ½ vanilla bean

Known locally as *pasta flora*, this dish is a direct relative of Italy's *pasta frolla*—meaning shortcrust pastry, the basis for tarts like this one. I've used plums in this recipe: they are beautiful and most commonly used in Cephalonia. Jams from almost any other fruit can be substituted. Use the best fruit available and in season.

Beat the butter and confectioners' sugar together until smooth. Beat in 1 egg and the vanilla extract. Add the flour, salt, and ground almonds and mix until a rough dough starts to form.

Turn out onto a lightly floured work surface and knead to a dough. Place on a floured tray, cover with plastic wrap, and refrigerate for 30 minutes.

Meanwhile, make the plum jam. In a heavy-based large deep saucepan, bring the plums, ½ cup (125 ml) water, and the lemon juice to a boil. Add the sugar and cook for 20 minutes.

Preheat the oven to 350°F (180°C) and grease a 10½ inch (26 cm) tart pan with a little butter.

Remove the pastry dough from the fridge and divide into two balls. On a lightly floured work surface, use a rolling pin to roll out one ball into a 12 inch (30 cm) circle.

Line the base of the tart pan with the pastry circle and spread 2 cups of the plum jam evenly over the base. Roll the other dough ball into a 10½ inch (26 cm) rectangle and cut into ¾ inch (2 cm) wide strips. Lay the pastry strips on top of the tart in a lattice pattern.

Beat the remaining egg and brush over the top of the tart to glaze. Bake the tart for 25 minutes until golden.

Meanwhile, to make the whipped cream, whisk the cream and sifted confectioners' sugar until stiff. Stir in the vanilla seeds.

To serve, cut the tart into slices and serve with the whipped cream.

Note
This recipe makes more jam than is needed for the tart. Store the extra jam in an airtight container in the refrigerator.

—*Serves 8*

ORANGE SPONGE CAKE *with* CANDIED GRAPES

Prep Time 15 minutes
Cooking Time 40 minutes

Sponge cake
4 tablespoons (2 oz/60 g) butter
2 tablespoons orange zest
1 cup (4½ oz/125g) all-purpose
    flour
1 pinch salt
4 eggs
Generous ½ cup (4½ oz/125 g)
    sugar

Candied grapes
9 oz (250 g) seedless grapes
1¼ cup (9 oz/250 g) sugar
⅓ oz (10 g) pectin
1 teaspoon lemon juice

Whipped cream
1 cup (250 ml) heavy whipping
    cream
1 tablespoon confectioners' sugar,
    sifted
Seeds from ½ vanilla bean

While an Italian pastry chef in the employment of a Genoese marquis in Spain is said to have invented the first sponge cake, the rest of the Western world has certainly embraced it. Greece is no exception, with numerous variations of the sponge cake, or *pantespani* as the Greeks call it, to be found throughout the country. As in this recipe, in Greece, sponge cake is usually served with some kind of syrup, and often with candied fruit, like these amazing grapes.

To make the sponge cake, first preheat the oven to 350°F (180°C).

Melt the butter and let it cool slightly. Grease a 9½ inch (24 cm) round cake pan with a little of the butter. Add the orange zest to the remaining butter.

Sift the flour and salt together into a bowl.

In a heat-resistant bowl, beat the eggs and sugar until pale.

Half-fill a saucepan with water and bring to a simmer over low heat. Place the bowl of eggs and sugar on top of the pan, ensuring the water does not touch the bottom of the bowl. Using an electric mixer, whisk for 10 minutes—the mixture should triple in volume.

Remove the bowl from the pan and sift in half the flour. Using a metal spoon, fold it in gently, then repeat with the remaining flour. Add the melted butter and orange zest and fold through again.

Pour the batter into the cake pan and bake for 25 minutes.

Meanwhile, to make the candied grapes, put the grapes, sugar, and a scant ¼ cup (50 ml) water in a pan and bring to a slow boil over low heat. Add the pectin and lemon juice and cook for around 10 minutes until it has a thick consistency: do not overboil.

To make the whipped cream, whisk together the cream and sifted confectioners' sugar until stiff peaks form. Stir in the vanilla seeds.

Remove the cake from the oven and cool on a rack. To serve, cut the cake into slices and serve with a tablespoon of candied grapes and whipped cream.

—Serves 8

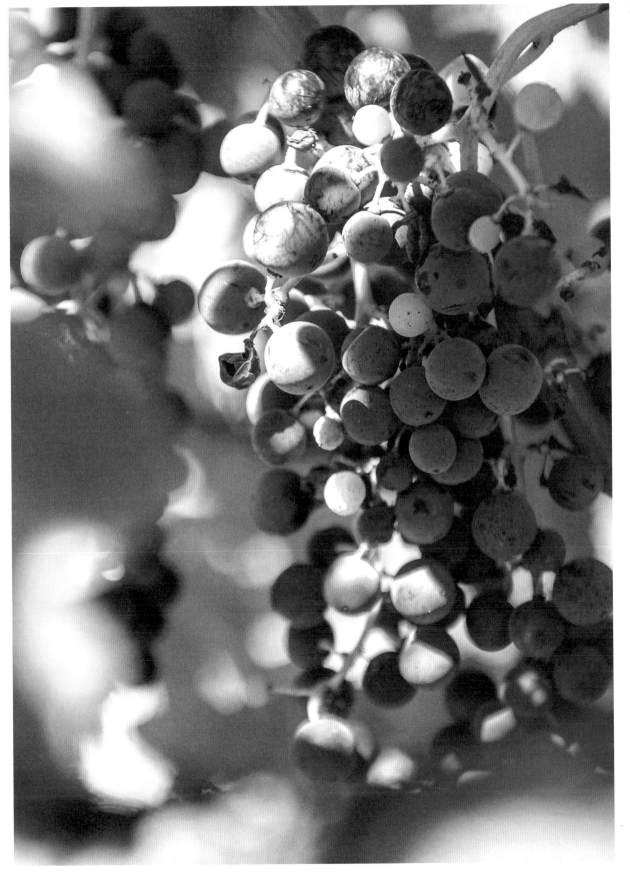

CORFIOT ALMOND AND GLACÉ KUMQUAT TORRONE

Prep Time 1 hour, plus 1 hour refrigeration
Cooking Time 15 minutes

4 cups (1 lb 5 oz/600 g) whole
  blanched almonds
7 oz (200 g) candied kumquats
  (or candied clementines or
  candied oranges)
¾ cup (9 oz/250 g) quality honey
2 egg whites
Seeds from 1 vanilla bean
2 cups (14½ oz/410 g) sugar
6 sheets of rice paper
7 oz (200 g) good-quality 55%
  dark chocolate (optional)

The word "torrone" or "nougat" in Greek is *mandolato,* and comes from the Venetian term *torrone mandorlato.* This recipe hails from Corfu, famous for both its kumquat cultivation and nougat production and features the amazing glacé kumquats produced on the island. Best enjoyed with an espresso, this torrone is delicious.

Preheat the oven to 350°F (180°C).

Place the almonds on a baking sheet and toast in the oven until golden brown. Keep in a warm place in the kitchen.

Drain the kumquats and remove any excess syrup. Slice the kumquats into ½ inch (1 cm) slices.

Place the honey in a small saucepan over medium heat and bring to 250°F (121°C) on a candy thermometer.

Using an electric mixer, beat the egg whites and vanilla seeds together until soft peaks form. Slowly pour the honey into the egg whites and beat until stiff peaks form. This is your meangue base.

Meanwhile, place a scant ½ cup (100 ml) water with the sugar in a small saucepan and bring up to 297°F (147°C). Slowly pour this into the meringue base until fully incorporated, firm, and glossy. Fold in the warm toasted almonds and kumquats.

Place 3 rice paper sheets, each about 9 × 6¼ inches (23 × 16 cm), on your work surface. Place a third of the mixture on each sheet, about ½ inch (1 cm) high. With a damp spatula, spread the mixture evenly. Cover each one with another rice paper sheet and gently press with a rolling pin. Place in the fridge for 1 hour until it hardens to nougat.

Brush a sharp bread knife with oil and slice into 3 x ½ inch (8 × 1 cm) pieces.

Gently melt the chocolate in a double boiler or in the microwave until just melted. Place in a pastry bag and drizzle over the nougat. Alternatively, dip whole pieces of the nougat into the chocolate or leave some nougat pieces without any chocolate glaze, for some variety.

Wrap the torrone in plastic wrap and store in an airtight container in the fridge for up to 3 weeks.

—*MAKES 54 pieces*

BASE
RECIPES

V

CHICKEN STOCK

Prep Time 15 minutes, plus 2–3 hours chilling
Cooking Time 2½–3 hours

2 lb 4 oz–2 lb 10 oz (1–1.2 kg)
  stewing chicken
2 lb 4 oz (1 kg) fresh chicken
  bones, thoroughly washed
3½ oz (100 g) carrot,
  roughly chopped
3½ oz (100 g) celery
  stalks, roughly chopped
3½ oz (100 g) leek,
  roughly chopped
3½ oz (100 g) onion,
  roughly chopped
3½ oz (100 g) Parmigiano
  Reggiano cheese
  rind (optional)
3 Italian parsley sprigs
Sea salt, to taste

Place all the ingredients in a large saucepan with 16 cups (4 liters) water and bring to a boil. Lower the heat and simmer, uncovered, for 2½–3 hours. Skim away the excess fat and other particles that come to the surface during the cooking process.

Remove the chicken, shred the meat for later use (discarding the skin and bones), strain the liquid through a fine strainer, and refrigerate for 2–3 hours or until it has a consistency similar to set jelly. Excess fat will solidify at the top of the refrigerated stock: remove this with a spoon and discard before using the stock.

Chicken stock can be made in advance and frozen in an airtight container for up to 2 months.

Note
The shredded chicken meat can be used in soups or pie fillings.

—*MAKES approximately 10 cups (2.5 liters)*

FISH STOCK

Prep Time 20 minutes
Cooking Time 1–1½ hours

3 tablespoons olive oil
3½ oz (100 g) carrot,
  roughly chopped
3½ oz (100 g) celery stalks,
  roughly chopped
3½ oz (100 g) leek,
  roughly chopped
3½ oz (100 g) onion,
  roughly chopped
4 lb 8 oz (2 kg) fresh snapper
  bones (including heads),
  washed thoroughly and
  roughly chopped
Scant ½ cup (100 ml) dry
  white wine
2 bay leaves
5 black peppercorns
3 Italian parsley sprigs
Sea salt, to taste

Heat the olive oil in a large saucepan over medium heat. Place all the vegetables in the saucepan and sauté until the leek and onion are soft and translucent. Add the fish bones and sauté for about 5 minutes, then add the wine. Cook until the wine has evaporated, then add 16 cups (4 liters) water, the bay leaves, peppercorns, parsley, and sea salt. Bring to a boil. Lower the heat and slowly simmer without a lid for 40 minutes. Skim away the excess fat and other particles that come to the surface during the cooking process.

Discard the larger fish bones and strain the liquid through a fine strainer. Pass again through a fine sieve or cheesecloth to make sure all the bones have been removed. Use the broth straight away or refrigerate.

Fish stock can be made in advance and frozen in an airtight container for up to 2 months.

—*MAKES approximately 15 cups (3.5 liters)*

VEGETABLE STOCK

Prep Time 20 minutes
Cooking Time ½–1 hour

Place all the ingredients in a large saucepan with 16 cups (4 liters) water and bring to a boil. Lower the heat and slowly simmer for 30–60 minutes. Pass through a fine sieve. Use the stock straight away or refrigerate.

Vegetable stock can be made in advance and frozen in an airtight container for up to 2 months.

—*MAKES approximately 12 cups (3 liters)*

7 oz (200 g) parsnip,
   roughly chopped
7 oz (200 g) turnip,
   roughly chopped
7 oz (200 g) carrots,
   roughly chopped
3½ oz (100 g) fennel bulb,
   roughly chopped
10½ oz (300 g) celery stalks,
   roughly chopped
7 oz (200 g) leek,
   roughly chopped
7 oz (200 g) onion,
   roughly chopped
1 bay leaf
2 thyme sprigs
2 Italian parsley sprigs
5 black peppercorns

BEEF OR VEAL STOCK

Prep Time 1½ hours, plus 2–3 hours chilling
Cooking Time 4½–5½ hours

Preheat the oven to 300°F (150°C).

Place the bones and trimmings in a roasting pan and roast until nicely browned (1–1½ hours). Heat the olive oil in a heavy-bottomed frying pan and sauté the onion, carrot, celery, and garlic until they are nicely browned.

Deglaze the roasting pan with a little water, then transfer to a large saucepan and add 16 cups (4 liters) water with all the other ingredients. Bring to a boil, then lower the heat and slowly simmer without a lid for 3–4 hours. Skim away the excess fat and other particles that come to the surface of the liquid during the cooking process. Strain the liquid through a fine strainer and refrigerate for 2–3 hours or until it has a consistency similar to set jelly. Excess fat will solidify at the top of the refrigerated stock. Remove this with a spoon and discard before using the stock.

Beef (or veal) stock can be made in advance and frozen in an airtight container for up to 2 months.

—*MAKES approximately 10 cups (2.5 liters)*

4 lb 8 oz (2 kg) fresh beef bones
   and trimmings (replace the beef
   bones with veal bones to make
   veal stock)
2 tablespoons olive oil
3½ oz (100 g) onion,
   roughly chopped
3½ oz (100 g) carrot,
   roughly chopped
3½ oz (100 g) celery stalks,
   roughly chopped
1½ oz (40 g) garlic cloves,
   roughly chopped
2 ripe tomatoes, roughly chopped
2 bay leaves
5 black peppercorns
2 thyme sprigs
2 Italian parsley sprigs

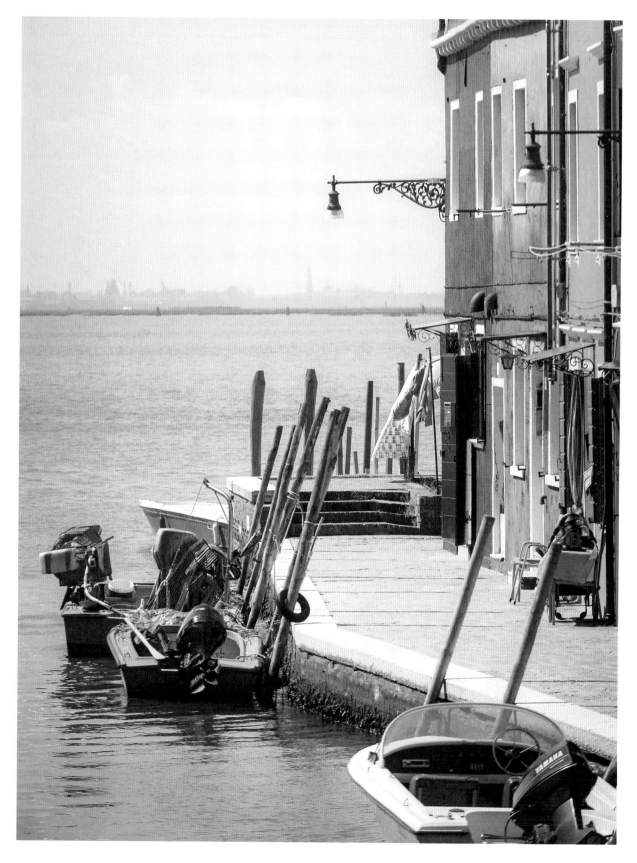

CRUSTACEAN BROTH

Prep Time 20 minutes
Cooking Time 1¼ hours

Preheat the oven to 350°F (180°C).

Place the shrimp shells in a small roasting pan and toss with the olive oil. Roast for 10–15 minutes or until golden, stirring occasionally.

In a large saucepan, heat the oil over medium–high heat and add the vegetables and garlic. Add the shrimp shells and tomato paste and sauté for 1 minute. Add the snapper bones and blue swimmer crabs and sauté for about 5 minutes before adding the white wine. Cook until the wine has evaporated, then add the tomatoes and 15 cups (3.5 liters) water. Bring the stock to a boil, then reduce to a slow simmer and cook for 40–60 minutes, skimming occasionally.

Discard the large fish bones and strain the liquid through a fine strainer. Make sure you press the shrimp shells while straining as they are full of extra flavor. Pass again through a fine sieve or cheesecloth to make sure all the bones are removed. Use the broth straight away or refrigerate.

Crustacean broth can be made in advance and frozen in an airtight container for up to 2 months.

—*MAKES approximately 12 cups (3 liters)*

10½ oz (300 g) shrimp shells
3 tablespoons olive oil
2½ tablespoons extra virgin olive oil
7 oz (200 g) onion, roughly chopped
5½ oz (150 g) carrot, roughly chopped
2 oz (60 g) celery stalks, roughly chopped
1½ oz (40 g) garlic cloves, roughly chopped
7 oz (200 g) tomato paste (concentrated purée)
4 lb 8 oz (2 kg) fresh snapper bones (including heads), washed thoroughly and roughly chopped
2 blue swimmer crabs (or any hard-shelled crabs), cleaned and cut into quarters
Scant ½ cup (100 ml) dry white wine
2 lb 10 oz (1.2 kg) ripe tomatoes, roughly chopped

FRESH EGG PASTA DOUGH

Prep Time 1 hour, plus 30 minutes chilling

2½ cups (11½ oz/330 g) all-purpose flour, plus extra for kneading and rolling
⅓ cup (2½ oz/70 g) fine semolina
½ teaspoon fine sea salt
4 free-range eggs

Combine the flour, semolina, and sea salt and place on a work surface or large wooden board in a peaked mound. With your hand, make a hole in the top of the mound so that it resembles a volcano. This hole needs to be big enough to house the eggs.

Break the eggs into the hole. Using your hands or a fork, gently beat the eggs, then mix in the flour. This is done by moving your hand in a circular motion, slowly incorporating the flour from the inside wall of the mound. Don't worry if it looks messy: this is normal. Once fully combined, knead a bit more flour into the dough if it feels wet or sticky. Set the dough aside and clean the work surface.

Dust flour onto the work surface and knead the dough for another 5 minutes. Wrap in plastic and refrigerate for at least 30 minutes.

To roll out the pasta, cut the rested dough into six 3½ oz (100 g) pieces. Flatten each piece with your hands, then begin passing the dough through a pasta machine, starting with the widest setting and then slowly reducing the width. This will make the pasta sheets increasingly thinner. The pasta sheets will appear quite rough at first, but as you pass them through the machine they will become more smooth. Pass the pasta through the machine at each setting at least twice.

After about the third setting, fold the pasta and pass it through the machine several more times, dusting with extra flour as necessary. It needs to be quite smooth. Folding also helps to create a flat edge to the pasta and, as you fold and pass it through, make sure that the dough is as wide as the rollers. This is especially important when pasta sheets are to be used for baked or filled pasta. Throughout this process it is important to dust the pasta sheets with a little extra flour. If the dough feels wet, increase the amount of flour used to dust the sheets. This will make a drier dough.

For flat pasta, such as pappardelle, tagliatelle, linguini, and spaghetti, it is important to dry the sheets a little prior to cutting them. This takes 5–45 minutes depending on humidity, temperature, and other weather conditions. If the sheets are cut while too wet, the pasta strips will stick together when drying or cooking. However, don't allow the pasta to dry out too much or it will break when cut.

The most basic pasta machines include cutting attachments for tagliolini and fettucine, and other attachments are sold for other types of pasta. Widths vary significantly from region to region. Here is an approximate guide:

- Capellini—1/16 inch (1–2 mm) wide
- Spaghetti and tagliolini—1/12 inch (2 mm) wide
- Linguini— 1/6 inch (4 mm) wide
- Tagliatelle—¼ inch (6 mm) wide
- Fettucine—⅓ inch (8 mm) wide
- Pappardelle—1¼ inch (30 mm) wide

—MAKES approximately 1 lb 5 oz (600 g)

SQUID (OR CUTTLEFISH) INK FRESH EGG PASTA DOUGH

Prep Time 1 hour, plus 30 minutes chilling

Combine the flour, semolina and sea salt and place on a work surface or large wooden board in a peaked mound. With your hand, make a hole in the top of the mound so that it resembles a volcano. This hole needs to be big enough to house the eggs.

Break the eggs into the hole. Combine the squid ink with 1 teaspoon water and add to the eggs. Using your hands or a fork, gently mix the ink and egg mixture, then slowly incorporate the flour. This can be done by moving your hand in a circular motion, slowly incorporating the flour from the inside wall of the mound. Don't worry if the dough looks like a mess: this is normal. Once fully combined, knead a bit more flour into the dough if it feels a little wet and sticky. Set the dough aside and clean the work space.

Dust flour onto the work surface and continue kneading the dough for 5 minutes. Wrap the dough in plastic and refrigerate for at least 30 minutes.

Roll the pasta to the desired thickness and cut into the desired shape (see Fresh Egg Pasta Dough opposite).

Note
Both squid and cuttlefish ink make good black pasta and can be substituted for each other. Ink products sold in jars are the most convenient source. However, you can obtain it from both fresh cuttlefish and squid as it is contained in the silver/black sacs inside the seafood. Extracting it will take a little practice, but it is a great source of ink.

—MAKES approximately 1 lb 5 oz (600 g)

2¼ cups (11½ oz/330 g) all-purpose flour, plus extra for kneading and rolling
⅓ cup (2½ oz/70 g) fine semolina
½ teaspoon fine sea salt
3 free-range eggs
2 tablespoons squid (or cuttlefish) ink

MAYONNAISE

Prep Time 15 minutes

Place the egg yolks, mustard, salt, and vinegar in a mixing bowl and then slowly whisk in the oil to emulsify. Store in an airtight container in the fridge for up to 1 week.

—MAKES 4¼ cups (1.1 liters)

6 egg yolks
1 tablespoon Dijon mustard
1 pinch salt
Scant ½ cup (100 ml) white wine vinegar
4 cups (1 liter) vegetable oil

HOMEMADE BUTTER/BUTTERMILK

Prep Time 30 minutes

3¾ cups (900 ml) heavy cream
1 tablespoon sea salt

To make butter, place the cream in a mixing bowl and whisk until the buttermilk separates from the butter solids.

Drain the buttermilk and reserve. You will be left with approximately 1¾ cups (14 oz/400 g) butter. Place the butter into a cheesecloth and rinse under cold running water until all the remaining buttermilk has been removed.

Wring the butter in a clean cheesecloth to remove as much of the remaining liquid as possible.

While the butter is still soft, mix in the salt in a dry mixing bowl and store in an airtight container in the fridge for 2–3 weeks.

—MAKES approximately 1½ cups (13 oz/360 g) butter

—MAKES approximately scant 2 cups (475 ml) buttermilk

MASCARPONE

Prep Time 5 minutes, plus cooling and overnight resting
Cooking Time 30–60 minutes

1 cup (250 ml) heavy cream
1 tablespoon lemon juice

Place the cream in a saucepan and, using a cooking thermometer, bring it to 190°F (88°C) over medium-high heat. When the cream is at temperature, lower the heat and maintain at 190°F (88°C).

Add the lemon juice to the cream and stir through until it thickens enough to coat the back of a wooden spoon.

Remove from the heat and allow to cool for 30 minutes.

Place three layers of cheesecloth inside a fine strainer and place over a bowl. When the mix is cold, pour into the strainer, then cover well and leave overnight.

Take the mascarpone out of the strainer and store in an airtight container in the refrigerator for up to 5 days.

—MAKES approximately scant ½ cup (3½ oz/100 g)

ACKNOWLEDGMENTS

Cookbooks are a massive undertaking and require the help and collaboration of a lot of people. I am deeply indebted to many and will attempt to name them all here. No doubt I will miss important people: I apologize in advance.

Firstly, thanks must start with Danielle Bowling, a ghost writer extraordinaire and very talented person who managed to put up with my scattered energy and historical "poetic license" like few would. Without her, this magnificent book simply wouldn't exist.

To Dean Worthy—The Restaurant Pendolino's head chef—another talented professional whose collaboration made creating this book a great pleasure. He was dragged halfway across the globe to complete the research and I am very grateful for the excellence of his work, often under trying circumstances. It is appreciated.

Mark Beattie, a dear friend and colleague, an industry professional, and fellow chef of the highest caliber, who really enabled me to do the crazy traveling and research that this book required. With tireless energy and an educated and keen critical eye, he is a person who only adds to the quality of any undertaking he is involved in. A first-rate human to boot. We are eternally grateful.

The teams at the restaurants: in particular Aimee, Maggi, Nic, Santosh, Loic, and many more. Lilet and Peter for helping with the recipe testing. Special thanks, again, to Raffaello Pignetti for the ongoing intellectual input that continues to color our days. To the non-executive restaurant team, Leon Young, John Malolakis, and Sam Kitchen, it goes without saying but the support is immensely appreciated.

To the two amazingly talented photographers: Andrea Butti in Italy, our location photographer, you're not family but you might as well be; and Alan Benson for such amazing studio shots. Gifted craftsmen.

Food stylist—Vanessa Austin, who's an absolute joy to work with. We're simply very grateful for the quality of the composition and for how quickly and enthusiastically you embraced this book's concept.

The team at Murdoch: Corinne Roberts, Vivien Valk, Jane Price, Kay Halsey, and Lou Johnson, a very big thank you for a great collaboration.

To the people on the ground in Venice and in the greater Venetian Republic. Firstly the wine producers— Degani, Cavazza, and La Farra—we are grateful for your long-standing support and the quality of what you do. To the Quintarelli family, thank you for so generously welcoming us into your extraordinary world. Time at Quintarelli is a sacred experience and is life changing for anyone truly interested in quality and craftsmanship. Grazie mille.

To some of the best restaurateurs in the business: the famous Mauro Lorenzon from L'Enoiteca Mascareta and Luca Di Vita from Osteria alle Testiere.

And to the Republic's Michelin culinary elite: Giancarlo Perbellini and the Alajmo brothers. These guys give cutting-edge context to an ever-evolving food culture in one of the most important culinary regions in the world. Extraordinary hospitality and enlightening dining experiences.

To Petros Markantonatos and the Gentilini family, from the Gentilini winery in Cephalonia. Spearheading the exciting "new" frontier in wine and food from the most ancient of lands, your help and guidance is deeply appreciated.

Nic, Pia, and Matilda in Milan. Thank you for the heartfelt friendship and shared passion for all things Italian, food, wine, and music, and for the last-minute bed after a 24-hour haul from Sydney—appreciated.

On the ground in Australia, special thanks to David Tsirekas, my "brother" from the "other" culture, and John Pye for the input on the recipes—much appreciated. Mitch and Mark, gratitude forever. To the crazy Veneta from Adelaide, Sandra Dei Poi—the support has been immense.

Thanks also to Luke Nguyen for the initial encouragement to become a cookbook author.

To my immediate and extended families—brothers, cousins, uncles, and aunties—the Zoccali and Prowse clans and to the Syrmis and Moraitis clans. The support is always felt and is always appreciated. A very special mention to my mother-in law, Maria Syrmis, and her family—my in-laws on Ithaca. I'm very grateful for the support, the memories, and the important input to this book.

And still on the subject of family, whilst not Venetian, my father, Domenico Zoccali, is an influence that lingers long and deep like a Giuseppe Quintarelli Amarone—grazie, papa.

Now for the three people who have really inspired this cookbook: Cristian, Ino, and Krissoula.

To Ino and Marianna Kuvacic, dear friends who have given much wisdom over many years, and context to the stunning place that is the Croatian coast. Thanks for your passion and enthusiasm and for seeding the concept of this book. You are inspiring people, deeply connected to your amazing history. It's a pleasure to know you and we are deeply grateful.

Cristian Casarin. Where do I start? Loud, passionate, loyal, knowledgeable, extremely funny, extremely Venetian—and strangely, a bloody Aussie too. The restaurant group sommelier, born in Noale, 30 kilometers from Venice but having made Sydney his home for some 20 years. We thank you for everything you've done; it's just been such a pleasure to do great work with you, and to do it together. Thanks also to your mom and dad, Mario and Rosalia, and for my favorite risotto of all time.

Krissoula, well, after 20 years of marriage here it is—Greece finally meets Italy in the most relevant of ways. Some have called you Penelope; I call you my beautiful, wise partner. And what a partnership. I love every bit of you, everything you believe in and stand for.

And now for the last two.

Thanks to my son, Luca, just for being who you are and for believing in your dad.

Lastly to my mother, Norma, for all the hard work and belief over many years: it will always be appreciated. The book is dedicated to you.

ACKNOWLEDGMENTS

INDEX

First American edition published 2020 by

INTERLINK BOOKS
An imprint of Interlink Publishing Group, Inc.
46 Crosby Street, Northampton, MA 01060
www.interlinkbooks.com

Published simultaneously in Great Britain and Australia by Murdoch Books,
an imprint of Allen & Unwin

Publisher: Corinne Roberts
American Edition Publisher: Michel Moushabeck
Editorial Manager: Jane Price
Creative Manager: Vivien Valk
Editor: Kay Halsey
American Edition Editor: Leyla Moushabeck
Designer: Lucy Sykes-Thompson
Location photography: Andrea Butti
Food photography: Alan Benson
Styling: Vanessa Austin
Food preparation for photography: Dean Worthy
Production Director: Lou Playfair
Production/US Edition: Jane Bugaeva

Library of Congress Cataloging-in-Publication data available
ISBN 978-1-62371-943-2

Color reproduction by Splitting Image Color Studio Pty Ltd, Clayton, Victoria
Printed by C & C Offset Printing Co Ltd, China